THE TRUTH-WALKER'S
JOURNEY

THE TRUTH-WALKER'S
JOURNEY

The UN-Becoming of Who You Are Not

HASEENA PATEL

Foreword by Dr. Sarbmeet S. Kanwal

PRAISE FOR THE TRUTH-WALKER'S JOURNEY

"If you have ever wondered who you are or why you are 'this way', this book can liberate you from the clutches of restrictive self-judgment. The teachings in The Truth-Walker's Journey are easy to recommend to others. It may even be an excellent workbook for groups growing together, or for families who wish to heal."
— **Henriette Alban, ND,**
  doctor of naturopathy; co-creator of *Conscious Evolution Dialogues*

"The pages touched my heart and awoke my soul's journey. This can and should become a life's resource workbook. This book is the perfect gift for loved ones."
— **Robin Cortese,**
  vice president & partner of AT&T Premier Technologies

"Isn't it so great when you find one of those books that invites you in, makes you question reality and validates that you are on the right path? This book immerses you into endless possibilities for both grounding and growth as you seek your truth, and it presents you with evidence to support you on your journey. Its value, along with yours is UN-Limited!"
— **Donna Palamar,**
  educator, youth empowerment coach, advisory board member of Leave No Girl Behind International

"Haseena offers practical, simple but challenging, transformational exercises for anybody to take on this exploration. I felt so supported along the way, and best of all, I felt like I had the right to surrender my insecurities and fears, my stories about myself."

— **Thomas Acklin, MD,**
regenerative neurologist, functional medicine physician

"The Truth-Walker's Journey: The UN-Becoming of Who You Are Not *offers a pragmatic path to co-creating peace and unity through finding inner truth, embracing the strength of our diversity and knowing that we each have a place at our collective table. The concrete exercises Haseena Patel invites us to do, lets the so needed sense of belonging Be-come brighter within – what a gift … thank you!"*

— **Drs. Anne-Marie Voorhoeve,**
evolutionary leader; co-founder of The Hague Center for Global Governance Innovation & Emergence; global creative strategy director of The Club of Budapest International Network; co-producer of World Unity Week, 99 Days of Peace through Unity and Peace Week 2020-2030

"Filled with skill and lived wisdom, this book is a welcoming guide through the layers that cloud us from our deepest truth – that we are each a radiant source of light, love, and caring that the world needs right now. Step onto the path of the Truth-Walker with Haseena to become your fullest self and create a life of inspired action and meaning."

— **Stephan Martin,**
director of the Deeptime Leadership Program

"This book is a fresh and actional guide. I use it daily in my work and in my personal healing from chronic pain. It's chock full of stories, practices, and exercises curated by this ground-breaking author and leader. I believe The Truth-Walker's Journey *has the power to unleash the creative abundance of our collective BE-ing."*

— **Lisa Verni,**
psychotherapist, creator of *Dancing with the Pain*, Deeptime leader and mentor, writer

"Haseena Patel, Congratulations on your masterpiece! It's amazing and your story, vision, and life purpose resonates fully in my heart. Truth is truth unless we are unable to perceive it. I am infinitely grateful for your courage to do your inner work – walk the path – so you can now lead the path. The Truth-Walker's Journey: The UN-Becoming of Who You Are Not is a must for anyone and everyone desiring to awaken to the light of their highest self. Bravo!"

— **Dr. Darren R. Weissman,**
the best-selling author of *The Power of Infinite Love & Gratitude* and Developer of The LifeLine Technique®

"Haseena's vast knowledge brings the reader to truly understand through analogies based on personal experiences and science, leading the reader to deeply understand the concepts within the journey's process. A truly amazing journey, in an amazing book, written by an amazingly talented writer and Truth-Walker!"

— **Catherine Woods, M.Ed., C.A.G.S., Ed.D.-ABD,**
director of student services, speaker, author

"I see Haseena's timeless wisdom as not us helping every individual reach the potential available to them, but I see it as a path for the cosmos to advance to its next level of unfolding."

— **Sarbmeet S. Kanwal, PhD,**
adjunct professor; TEDx speaker; lead teacher of Deeptime Networks

"'By bringing our individuality to the table, we create possibilities for our world which didn't exist before.' Haseena Patel states in The Truth-Walker's Journey.

"That's a worthy purpose for each of us seeking a meaningful life – that is all of us. Haseena's courage in sharing her journey inspires us to challenge ourselves to join her in pursuing the person beneath the personality."

— **Martha D. Humphreys,**
Emmy Award winner, writer, producer, Memoir Maven

©2023 by Haseena Patel

Published by

Healing Breakthrough University
South Africa

All rights reserved. This book or parts thereof may not be reproduced or transcribed in any form or by any means, mechanical or electronic, including photocopying and recording, or by any information storage and retrieval system, without prior written permission from the publisher, other than the inclusion of brief quotations embodied in articles and reviews.

Note to the reader:
The information and advice contained in this book are based upon the research and the personal and professional experiences of the author. There are no contra-indications for or side effects of reading this book. Please do not consult with your physician. Instead, claim personal sovereignty, align with your truth and take to heart what feels right for you. Yes, you have the power and you have the answers.

For information about special discounts available for bulk purchases, contact Healing Breakthrough University at info@healingbreakthroughuniversity.com.

Paperback ISBN: 978-0-6397-8788-6

Editing by Martha D. Humphreys
Book design by YellowStudios

First Edition

To

My partner, my teacher, my lover, my ever-reacher journey-mate, in all THings verbal and UN-verbal. Thank you for BE-ing wiTH me, Tom.*

---

* The capitalised "TH" isn't a typo – it's a reference I share with my partner. "BE-ing" isn't a typo either. It has become part of my lingo and I use it throughout the book as a reminder that we are each a process of evolution and ever evolving – each of us in our human and non-human global family is a verb, not a noun. We have a choice in what BE-ing is, and that choice is empowering. The capitalised "UN-" also forms part of the lingo of this book, as you may have guessed from the subtitle.

TABLE OF CONTENTS

Foreword by Dr. Sarbmeet Kanwal xv

Introduction 1

PART 1: TRUTH WITHIN 5

    Chapter 1: UN-Defining Truth 7

    Chapter 2: The Energy of Truth 13

    Chapter 3: Why Your Truth Matters 19

    Chapter 4: This Is Your Journey 23

PART 2: AWARENESS 25

    Chapter 5: The Story of Your Life 27

    Chapter 6: The Moments of the Story Woven Together 31

    Chapter 7: The Five Motivators 35

    Chapter 8: The Nine Base Fears 39

    Chapter 9: Why Fear Has Your Back Daily 43

    Chapter 10: The Awakening 45

    Chapter 11: The Significant Moment 47

    Chapter 12: The Big, Scary (Fill In The Blank) 51

    Chapter 13: Let the Journey UN-Fold 55

    Chapter 14: Gratitude 57

Chapter 15: Letting Go 59

Chapter 16: The Ride of Your Life 61

Chapter 17: You Don't Scare Me Anymore 63

Chapter 18: Moving Out of No Man's Land 67

PART 3: JOURNEY OF SEEKING 71

Chapter 19: Your Quest 73

Chapter 20: The Journey Begins 81

Chapter 21: Accessing Your Travel Gear 87

Chapter 22: Your Choice 91

Chapter 23: Claiming Sovereignty 93

Chapter 24: Applying the Shift Within 97

Chapter 25: The Essence of the Seeking 101

PART 4: UN-BECOMING 105

Chapter 26: The Fullness of BE-ing Empty 105

Chapter 27: UN-Becoming Defined 109

Chapter 28: Red Zone or Rebirth Zone 111

Chapter 29: The UN-Becoming Process 115

Chapter 30: Breaking Through the Belief System
of Feeling Unworthy 127

Chapter 31: Six Keys to Manifesting Truth 133

Chapter 32: Creating a New Default in 30 Days 139

Chapter 33: Honouring Your BE-ing 143

PART 5: BE-ING 149

Chapter 34: The Truth-Walker's Manifesto 151

Chapter 35: Principle 1: The Awakening 153

Chapter 36: Principle 2: The Journey 157

Chapter 37: Principle 3: The BE-ing 161

Chapter 38: Principle 4: The Freeing 165

Chapter 39: Principle 5: The "Healing to" 169

Chapter 40: Principle 6: The Embracing 173

Chapter 41: Principle 7: The Recognising 177

Chapter 42: Principle 8: The Contributing 181

PART 6: GIVING 185

Chapter 43: Dear Truth-Walker 185

Chapter 44: Trust 189

Chapter 45: You and the Collective 191

Chapter 46: The Thought-Shift 195

Chapter 47: The Last Question 197

Gift for You 199

Continue the Adventure – Join the Tribe 199

Acknowledgements 201

About the Author 205

FOREWORD

In a world besieged by deepening conflicts and rising injustice, Haseena Patel's *The Truth-Walker's Journey* comes to us as a shining ray of hope. In a book filled with practical, hands-on guidance, she leverages her own journey of discovery and transformation to offer a step-by-step handbook to first help each of us realize our own deep-seated truth and then align our life with it. Peppered with real-life examples, journaling exercises, reflection pauses, and chapter-end summaries, this book will become your live-in, personal coach whose counsel you can seek at your own convenience and pace.

The context in which I met Haseena a little more than a year ago, is as cosmic as the task she has taken on in this book – helping humans connect with their inner truths. She was on a path to being certified as a cosmic deep time leader through learning to apply the story of our origin to the expression of her allurements. I was aiding in the teaching of the Deeptime Leadership and Personal Empowerment certification course. I was assigned to mentor her certification project which, it turned out, was creating a course based on the teachings of this book. It is my faith in her work that has me writing a foreword to *The Truth-Walker's Journey* now.

In helping every individual reach their potential, Haseena's timeless wisdom is advancing the unfolding of the cosmos. Cosmic evolution is an ongoing cyclic process. Each level starts by creating variations within whatever it is that is emerging at the leading edge of development. This diversity allows for creative engagement between the differentiated parts to bring about a new whole that is surprisingly fresh and brimming with future promise. Joining three different particles (electron, proton, and neutron) enables the cosmos to create atoms. Many different kinds of stars come together to build fertile galaxies. A variety of atoms link up to make life-generating molecules. Many cell types work together to form complex organisms and a diverse set of species must interact to establish prospering eco-systems.

While the interexchange between all parts of the biosphere must continue for our species to survive, a new kind of interconnection between humans (a noosphere) is needed to move evolution to its next natural level. Haseena's book makes it clear that such a communion can only be fruitful if we engage with the energy of our very own, inborn, personal truths that bring to bear the potential that we each carry within us. These truths carry our personal stamps for this very reason, so that the union created out of this diversity can be abundant in its bounty, astounding in its promise, and boundless in its potential.

Why is it so difficult to tune into our personal truths and live our lives while standing up for who we really are? As Haseena points out, the forces that want us to conform to traditional practices and adhere to cultural norms are exceedingly strong. Hierarchical structures and acquiescence to authority continue to play large roles in our societies. This is being increasingly added to by the power exerted by unscrupulous corporations and exploitative media. The latest assault on our individuality comes from the rampant adoption of social media by young and eager minds seeking instant popularity. What we need to stay strong in the face of a rising tide of oppressive influences is a strong ally by our side, one who is well versed in the wisdom of the ages. This is exactly what Haseena offers us in the guise of *The Truth-Walker's Journey* guidebook.

What do we really mean by the truth within us that we need to align with? If the concept feels a little unclear, all you need to do is read the book. What Haseena means by this truth becomes increasingly clear as she delves into every aspect of this idea. Our truth is who we are from the inside; it is the essence of our psyche. It is what is left when all the influences trying to corrupt it are taken away. Our truth is what we have been endowed with to enable us to express our divinity. It is what makes our hearts sing the song of love. It is the force that can free us from all fear. It is the flame in us that we cannot allow anyone to snuff out.

If you are ready to start co-creating your life from the truth that you ARE, then read on. Your future awaits you!

Sarbmeet S. Kanwal, PhD

Adjunct Professor; Lead Teacher, Deeptime Networks; Board Member, Monmouth Center for World Religions and Ethical Thought; Founder/Coordinator, MOSAIC youth program; TEDx speaker

INTRODUCTION

Have you ever been told NO? That you don't belong, that you're not capable, that it's "not your place to"? We have that in common. For most of my life I listened to the message I was given that I didn't own my body, that my mind should be used for what was deemed by *"respected society, culture, community, and elders of spiritual traditions"* to be morally right, and that my soul's journey was not of my own choosing. I bought into what I was told – that nothing about my life belonged to me and that I didn't matter.

If these prison bars are yours too, but your heart is screaming, "That's not true. That is not who I am inside!" I invite you to listen to those screams. And I extend the invitation to the journey in these pages – will you go on the quest to UN-Become who you are not so that you can live the truth of who you are?

You are capable, you are worthy, and the journey to be YOU is worth your time. Only you get to decide who you are or what your journey is about. I started to love myself for the wholeness and nakedness of who I am when I discarded the trappings of opinions, definitions, expectations and dreams FOR and ABOUT me.

I reached the point of: "F***, NO! You don't get to define me. No one does. Only *I* define who I am and what my life is about!" This anger was the birthplace of individuality. I healed to my next evolutionary level, recognising my interconnectedness with my world as well as the enormous value I contributed when living on my own terms. My "us-and-them" mentality dissolved. From a deep-seated duality, I evolved to embrace our ONE-ness.

Whatever your starting point, your journey is important. Choose YOU because who you are is enough. You matter. There is a saying that you should "speak your truth even when your voice shakes". I support you in doing that. I grew up non-white in Apartheid South Africa, and often wondered how different the life of every South African would be if we all spoke our truths back then. Back to YOU – your voice doesn't have to shake. Through your journey you will become so powerfully YOU that the light of who you are will illuminate the shadow you perceive right now. Darkness is nothing more than the absence of light.

The light of your self-worth has the power to dissolve your fears and every thought, word and action about or towards you that isn't in alignment with who you are.

Read the sentence in bold again – it speaks volumes. The Truth-Walker's Journey is about finding YOU in the sea of voices around you. It is about getting quiet and listening, then recognising and removing the white noise.

Are you ready?

Are you willing to take the first step and be open to the limitlessness of who you are?

Are you open to acknowledge your interconnectedness with our beautiful Mother Earth and our Universe? That's right – you are not alone.

The truth is that you are UN-stoppable, UN-limited and UN-deniably strong. You are an expression of the Universe and you were birthed by Mother Earth herself. The question is: what will you choose…right now…in this very moment? The power of choice is everything!

If you choose to go on this journey of UN-Becoming, there is a good chance we will connect beyond the pages of this book. I look forward to it.

Namaste.

Haseena

Part 1:
TRUTH WITHIN

Your truth is born from the contrast of who you are not.

One of my most profound memories is an incident that happened when I was about twelve years old. I was on the tennis ladder at school and was one of the students called on to be a ball-girl when our nationally seeded tennis players came to our little town for a competition. Let me fill you in on the background: it was 1988 in Apartheid South Africa and I was non-white. I wouldn't have been asked at all but I was a student at the only private school in our town and it was run by Dominican Sisters. How things worked was that when there were big events like these, students from all the "white" schools in the town would have been included while "non-white" schools were never considered. Our private school had to be included as a formality although we were a multi-racial school.

I was caught up in the excitement, even though something felt off about entering the "whites only" athletics club where the event was held. I was one of the ball-girls for the match between two men – a gentleman who had a winning attitude, and a really sore loser whose attitude left a lot to be desired. Halfway through the match, the sore loser suddenly reported to the umpire that I was distracting him by moving and talking to my friend on the other side of the court. I hadn't moved and certainly had not talked to anyone. I had the sickening feeling that the sore loser accused me because I was an easy target – the only non-white child on the court. The umpire didn't buy the man's story and the match continued. The gentleman won. He thanked all of us and it seemed that I was the only one who heard and looked in his direction. He said thank you again – I was still so shaken by the loser's unfair accusation that I didn't have the presence of mind to reply to the gentleman.

I internalised the feeling of that memory without even knowing it. Somewhere along the way, feelings like this in many different contexts became part of a belief system that began to chafe away at the knowing of who I was inside. The premise of the belief system was: *who I am is wrong*.

While that was the belief that caused me to stray furthest away from my deepest sense of self, it was also the belief that caused me to hit the place people call rock bottom; the place where you find yourself asking or praying or begging whatever seems to be out there in the Great Beyond – *please help me, I want to live, please help me to get out of this black hole, please help me to give what's inside of me because I know I have something to give*.

That moment becomes your beginning. And the place that seems so hopeless and black, the contrast of who you are not, becomes the opening from where you have acknowledged the Light of your BE-ing, your truth, and given it permission to start shining through.

Chapter 1
UN-DEFINING TRUTH

*Truth: the deepest sense of self, the Light of one's
BE-ing*

Truth is the alignment between your outward behaviour, words, thoughts and actions, and that deepest part of yourself that is peace, love, contentment and a connection to something greater.

It is the feeling when your outward characteristics and behaviour match up to who you are inside, and that "matching up" creates a feeling that all is well.

How to tell what your truth is and isn't

We communicate daily through our thoughts, words and actions. Not all our communication (even with ourselves) is truth-based.

How do you tell the difference between <u>thoughts</u> that are truth-based and those that are not?

- Thoughts that are aligned with your truth are heart-centred.
- You feel the resonance of such communication and you feel good or relieved.
- These thoughts are purposeful and solution-oriented.

In contrast:

- Thoughts that reflect untruths are often accompanied by emotional swings.
- They are undirected and sporadic.
- There is no solution or way to move forward rooted in these thoughts.
- These thoughts leave one feeling helpless and disempowered.
- When shame, anger or guilt accompanies a thought about yourself or your experience, that thought cannot be heart-centred and is therefore not aligned with your truth.

How do we tell the difference between <u>words</u> that are truth-based and those that are not?

- Unkind words carry an energy that does not feel heart-centred. Unkindness is a learned behaviour and is not natural to who you are.
- When you berate yourself or anyone else, those words and the energy of those words are not heart-centred, they are ego-filled. Your ego is not aligned with the truth of who you are.

Are all positive thoughts truth-aligned while all negative thoughts are based on untruths?

Thoughts simply ARE. We give them the 'positive' or 'negative' attachment.

Sometimes truth-aligned thoughts are epiphanies that may sadden you on some level, but still feel aligned with your deepest sense of self. These epiphanies give you a sense of purpose and direction. You feel valued, worthy, empowered, and sometimes relieved, despite the pain.

Thoughts that are not aligned with your truth feel hollow and superficial – you may be saying a positive affirmation aloud while the words and energy of this affirmation don't align with who you are or your purpose. You don't believe the words. There is an accompanying feeling of wanting to stay in the moment so that the bubble doesn't burst – you work hard not to allow anything negative into your space that will change this superficial positive thought.

The difference between truth and honesty

Honesty is the state of how you feel in a particular moment. It is based on your emotions and is not necessarily aligned with the deepest part of who you are. For example, when someone you care about hurts you through their words or actions, if you are being honest, you might say: "I wish you hadn't come into my life!" Your response is honest and based on how you feel at that moment, however, it is ego centred. When you are aligned with your Inner BE-ing, you know your truth – the person came into your experience for a purpose, and their words and actions are part of *their* life journey, not yours. Your experience with them presents a choice as to what your thoughts, words and actions will be in this moment – this choice is *your* truth and part of *your* life journey.

The individual nature of truth

Many of us have been raised with the idea that truth is a universal constant – something solid, stable and exactly the same for every individual. However, each of us is a filter of what we observe. That alone makes our truths individual. And if the way we perceive things is different, then our feelings about these perceptions cannot be the same. Throw in upbringing and environmental influences, and our truths differ substantially.

Go outside tonight and look at the moon if it is visible. The same moon can be observed by people in different parts of the world. The moon is a constant, but where we observe it from and the angle at which we observe it makes it appear different to each of us. As a result, the truth of how the moon appears to each of us is individual.

Now imagine driving to a friend's home on the other side of town – look at the moon from this angle. Your experience will be different even though it is still the same moon observed by the same person. Since no two experiences can ever be the same, even if the same universal truth applied in a situation, both experiences would be interpreted differently by you.

Since there is always an observer present to bear witness to and interpret any event or situation, and no two experiences are the same even when experienced by the same observer, there can be no universal truth that we can all subscribe to.

The science behind the individuality of truth

There is an experiment in quantum physics (the double slit experiment) which demonstrates that the mere presence of an observer changes the behaviour of electrons. There are various theories explaining the reasoning for this phenomenon – one theory hypothesises that the equipment the observer has set up to observe the experiment may be responsible for interference in the experiment, while another claims that the energy field of the observer has influenced the behaviour of the electrons. All theories concur that the observer plays a role in the results of the experiment.

Even to verify that such an experiment was done with the necessary requirements, an observer has to be present. Would the experiment have any meaning if there was no observer present to observe and interpret the results?

The dual nature of your existence

You are not solely the participant or "main character" of your existence. Nor are you merely an observer.

You, as observer, are a participant in every situation you observe. *You* make the situation meaningful according to your own thoughts, feelings and life experience. In other words, you become a filter and bring to the situation an energy that affects those around you. Your truth has a ripple effect on your world.

What would happen if you were to change your thoughts in any specific moment, and feel differently about a situation? In that moment, your energy would have changed, your interpretation of the situation would have altered, and that which was being observed would also be different for you.

You are the creator of what you observe. You have the power to create change; you have the ability to shape your world.

Your power to create change

Your observation of an experience is filtered by your interpretation, and your interpretation begins with your power of thought.

Have you ever watched a movie or read a book or had a conversation that touched you so deeply that you were brought to tears? This is an example of a situation that is observed and interpreted by you, and your thoughts and feelings were so strong that they caused a physical reaction.

Here is another example – close your eyes and imagine this situation:

- You have a lemon in your hand – see it…feel it…smell it.
- Take a plate and a knife, and cut the lemon into the plate.
- Pick up one of the lemon halves.
- Hold it close to your nose and inhale the smell deeply.
- Then take a big bite out of the lemon.

What is the strongest sensation that you are experiencing? Are you salivating? You've proved that your thoughts have the power to create physical results.

Chapter 2
THE ENERGY OF TRUTH

When a tiny pebble is dropped in a pond, the ripple it creates shifts the whole world a fraction. The world is different in the smallest of ways, but the fact is that it is different. Likewise, our truths create ripples in our lives, in the lives of those closest to us, and in the world. Our truths have an energy more powerful than we can imagine. They are the driving force behind whatever we do and how we view ourselves, our lives and the world in general. We see things according to the energy that we carry; we create our own world through that which we see and the energy we send out in response to it.

When a truth has been spoken, those words have carried within them the seeds of the energy of that truth. It is not the words themselves that hold the power, but the energy with which they are given to the world. Words should not be feared, but considered carefully. The same words spoken by two people may carry a different energy and a different intention. The same words heard by two people will have a different meaning for each of them, and they will each respond with an energy according to their personal interpretation of those words.

There's a school of thought that says you must not speak what you don't want. That you must not give words to it, for words are powerful and the beginning of any creation. But it is not the words, the symbols on paper, that hold the power – words are merely representations of the energy you are carrying about that particular aspect of life. By ignoring that which you fear, by simply not giving words to it, you are not removing the feeling in your heart – the fear itself.

Once words are written down, the fears they represent become smaller. You have reduced the fears to miniature representations. You have liberated the truth of where you are, and once liberated, the fear component of that truth cannot fester and eat you up inside. You have acknowledged and dared to deal with the fear, and you will finally be free. You know where you are, and you can direct yourself to where you need to go. Only when you admit how you feel, is it possible to reach for a better thought. Reframing can only be done once you know what it is that you want to reframe.

- It is only once you say the word "death" that you can reframe it and view it as "re-birth".
- It is only when you acknowledge the truth that this may be the end that you can start seeing it as the beginning of something new.
- Fear is an opportunity to explore options; to reach for better thoughts.

It is empowering to liberate your truth – YOU have the opportunity to collaborate with your feelings instead of your unsaid fears and insecurities controlling your thoughts.

READER'S THOUGHT QUEST:

- What thought about yourself or an experience have you had in the last three hours that felt aligned with who you are?
- What thought about yourself or an experience have you had in the last three hours that felt superficial?

(It's okay if you don't recognise what thoughts you've had that feel aligned or superficial. From this point on, start observing your thoughts.)

ACTION SESSION:

Requirements: A journal and a pen

- In your journal, write one thought about yourself that feels aligned with your truth right now.
- Write one thought about yourself that feels untrue or as if you're being unfair to yourself.
- Write an affirmation, if any, that feels untrue for you right now.

EXAMPLE:

- Truth-aligned thought: I have allowed the clutter in my office to spiral into chaos because if I kept everything in order, I would have enough free time and would feel organised enough to face my fear of failure.
- Thought that feels hollow or untrue: I am incapable of achieving my goal because I am not worthy of it.
- Affirmation that feels untrue: I am a billionaire.

OBSERVATION:

- Think about each point you listed above. Say each thought and the affirmation aloud and notice how you feel when you say each of them. Take a minute for each and feel your way through it.

THE TAKE-HOME:

Truth isn't about the words you use. It is about the energy of those words and how that energy resonates with the truth of who you are at that particular moment.

Truth, words and interactions

The same goes for the spoken word – it is also just a representation. But the spoken word (presuming you're not talking to yourself!) has a certain power of its own because it involves communication between two or more people who interpret things differently. Share the words that come from deep within your soul with the special people who will treat those words, the offerings of your soul, with love and care.

The metaphor of ocean waves illustrates this principle well. When two waves meet, there is one of three results.

- One result may be that superposition occurs – the waves simply pass through each other and continue as before without disturbing each other.
- The second result can occur when the crest of one wave meets the trough of another. The waves cancel each other out, and we call this destructive interference. They have destroyed each other in the process of interacting.

- The third possible result is constructive interference. The crest of one wave connects with the crest of another wave (or the trough of one wave meets the trough of another) and in their collision, the resulting wave is bigger and more powerful – it is the total of the two waves that gave birth to it.

The energy of the spoken word has a certain power because it is energy coming from your BE-ing interacting with energy from another BE-ing. The collective energy during that communication is not your energy alone. It is important to ensure that this collective energy is inspiring and uplifting so that it serves you well in your journey forward. Avoid speaking your truth to someone whose energy is going to result in destructive interference in that moment.

Chapter 3
WHY YOUR TRUTH MATTERS

We are at a time in our history where we cannot draw on experience to help us. The internet redefines our world; we are in the fourth industrial revolution, as well as a collective redefining of the meaning of freedom and life-purpose. People are standing up for their personal truths at great cost to themselves. We're developing more courage and resilience as a world, and there are more possibilities than ever for each of us.

At the same time, polar opposites engulf us. The same technology developments that unite our world beyond borders and boundaries, allow us to become physically isolated – all we need is a cell phone and we can communicate at low cost with people around the world while ignoring everything and everyone in our immediate vicinity. We can give a new meaning to mass action with online movements that draw in millions of people, however we are functioning at a high price. We sacrifice good food for fast foods that require minimal time to prepare; we go through tons of plastic that ends up in landfills; we use the fastest forms of transportation, causing unnecessary pollution, to support the difference we want to make. In short, we betray the trust of our non-human global family (our biosphere and geosphere) and destroy our relationship with Mother Earth in the process of "advancement". We are constantly weighing the odds as to whether it's justified or what the most moral choice would be.

To make these decisions, we're using universal guidance or belief systems which don't provide us with answers to the questions we have currently. We continue asking the external to define right and wrong for us when decisions made because of politics and power don't encompass the context or well-being of our world today. We still don't have any answers and we're giving away our personal sovereignty in exchange for a controlled narrative.

Let's face it: the foundations and structures that were once built to protect and guide us in various ways are disintegrating. Bastions like justice systems, cultures and traditions no longer serve us. As the world becomes more expansive for us and more fluid (with communication and relationships extending beyond the boundaries of our communities, countries, our planet and even our dimension), we no longer feel bound by these "protective" walls. Our ties are being slowly severed and we have a glimpse of complete freedom. Most of us respond with complete insecurity. Without our structures, who are we and what is our purpose? We have never completely relied on ourselves to answer these questions...until now. The prospect is as exciting as it is frightening. Many cling desperately to the falling rocks of their crumbling belief systems, afraid that they will crumble, too. People are searching for hope around them when that sense of hope is within – it is ever present in their deepest sense of self, the Light of their BE-ing, their truth.

READER'S THOUGHT QUEST:

- What beliefs have you learned in your life that you no longer embrace?
- If you could live exactly as you choose, what would be different in your life?

ACTION SESSION:

Requirements: A journal and a pen

- In your journal, write three things that you'd like to change in your life so that you feel more in alignment with the truth of who you are.
- For each point above, list one way in which your life would be different if you changed that particular thing.
- Now write the first step you could take to make each change.

EXAMPLE:

- What I'd like to change: I'd like to stop smoking.
- How my life would be different: My health would improve.
- The first step: Figure out why I smoke.

OBSERVATION:

- Take notice of why the three things on your list came to mind first – do they rank as high-priority changes?

THE TAKE-HOME:

This session is about exploring possibilities. It is not about putting pressure on yourself to change anything yet. You are discovering what your truth is, why you'd like to live your truth and what change you could make by doing so. The "how to" will come later with a process that will help you make these changes if you so desire.

Chapter 4
THIS IS YOUR JOURNEY

The Truth-Walker's Journey is a journey of the sense of self and the realisation that there is no one universal truth; there is no structure that can save us or tell us what to do or make our broken moral compasses work.

Source (call it God within, Universe, Divine Presence, Higher Self, your centre, your heart, or whatever resonates with you) guides the truth of every BE-ing. We are individuals in our need for connection and how we define and understand this connection, as much as our DNA, fingerprints and life experiences are unique and individual to each of us. Therefore, there can be no ONE universal truth that guides ALL of us and that we all 'fit' into.

The irony is that the more integrated we become as a global community, the more we observe our individuality and uniqueness, and the more we realise that our individual truths are the only reliable source of guidance.

We are all interconnected – as global citizens of, from and on Mother Earth, and in the Heavenly realm (on a Soul plane). How we choose to connect and how we observe the connection is individual. By bringing our individuality to the table, we create possibilities for our world which didn't exist before. Our strength as a collective is in our diversity.

In other words, this is YOUR journey and you get to gift the world with your presence as a Truth-Walker if you so choose.

Part 2: AWARENESS

Every one of us has a story – an explanation of the events of our lives; an interpretation of who we are and how we got here. We weave this story from the fabric of our individual observations and interpretations of our unique experiences. Motivators, fears, truths and distortions drive our story.

The journey of the Truth-Walker is an exploration of that story, and going beyond the story; UN-telling your story to reach the point of everything that is YOU – the point where awareness meets the truth of your soul.

As a Truth-Walker, you will find your way of BE-ing aligned with Divinity; a space that isn't governed by fear or society's demands. Your way forward becomes the path that resonates with your soul.

Right now you are at the point of awareness – the exploration of your story begins here.

Let's go deeper.

Chapter 5
THE STORY OF YOUR LIFE

Throughout our lives, we carry with us moments of significance that we feel have shaped us. When we make choices or face different situations in daily life, we call these significant moments into our awareness and use them as a yardstick by which to measure the value of our present experiences or as a way of predicting the outcome of future experiences.

In theory, this appears to be an effective system. Here is why this system is flawed:

- If you were not living in alignment with the truth of your soul during your moments of significance, you cannot use their outcome as an indicator of what your thoughts, words and actions should be in the present – your yardstick is skewed towards the misaligned YOU of the past.

- In the past, you saw things through a different lens because you might have believed different things about yourself and your world. Since then you have evolved and, even if you were aligned with your truth in the past, you would no longer have the same outlook if the same event took place in your present.

Begin to explore your moments of significance – think about the questions in the *Reader's Thought Quest,* move on to the *Action Session* and *Observation* using your pen and journal, then take note of *The Take-Home.*

READER'S THOUGHT QUEST:
- Think of the significant moments in your life – which moments jump out at you immediately?
- Do you perceive the significant moments in your life as positive or negative?
- What makes each of these moments significant?
- Would you want to have another shot at any of these significant moments and change their outcome?

ACTION SESSION:
Requirements: A journal and a pen

Become aware of your life as you see it right now. To do this, write at least five significant moments of your life in point form (it doesn't matter whether those events seem positive or negative to you). Then write your feelings or impressions of each event.

For example, you might write:

- I won a writing contest at school when I was twelve and no one in my family attempted to be there when I received the award. (Feelings: hurt, I didn't matter, no one cared.)
- I bought my first car when I was twenty years old after working two jobs and attending college at the same time. (Feelings: proud of myself, empowered.)

OBSERVATION:

- Read what you just wrote. Pretend you're reading the events of someone else's life, Do you feel uncomfortable, have a sinking feeling in your stomach, or feel amazed at having lived through these events? Do you have any other powerful feelings about these events?
- Examine your feelings and record them on paper.

THE TAKE-HOME:

You have either discovered or consolidated the events of your life that made an impression on you. You also know your emotions associated with each event.

Chapter 6
THE MOMENTS OF THE STORY WOVEN TOGETHER

Just as you sew different patches of fabric into a quilt, you have woven your significant moments into the story of your life.

When you pick up this piece of fabric of your life, composed of significant moments, what do you see?

READER'S THOUGHT QUEST:
- From the events above, what is your story and does it reflect who you are inside?
- How does your story make you feel – happy, sad, angry, a combination of emotions?
- Do you perceive your story as positive or negative?
- If you could relive your life, would your story be different? If so, how?
- Are you at peace with the story of your life?

ACTION SESSION:

Requirements: A journal and a pen

- Write your story, as you see it, in a paragraph. If you'd rather make a video or audio recording of yourself telling your story, do so.

- Beneath your story, write the feelings that came to you while telling your story.

OBSERVATION:

- Pretend you're reading the story of someone else's life, and read what you just wrote. Do you feel uncomfortable, have a sinking feeling in your stomach, or feel amazed at this story?

- Examine your feelings and record them.

- Does the **story** of your life hold more emotion for you than the **events** (significant moments) of your life in the previous exercise?

THE TAKE-HOME:

The events of your life do not define you. They simply are. YOU attach the accompanying emotions, YOU hold the power of thought, and YOU choose your interpretation.

Were you wronged?

Were you treated like a hero?

Were you treated like you weren't even there?

No matter what happened to you, you hold the 'significance' card.

You have the power to say: "No event defines my life!" or, if applicable, "This is my moment to shine!" No matter what the events are, it is up to you to give them meaning.

It is YOU who counts.

Only *you* have defined you, and that definition may or may not reflect the truth of who you are. *You* have the power to live your story powerfully, or to change it.

Chapter 7
THE FIVE MOTIVATORS

Every individual wants to:

- Know they matter
- Belong
- Express their individuality
- Feel fulfilled
- Make their pain stop

Sometimes, in desperation, we are so focused on one or more of the five motivators in a situation that we consciously or unconsciously come from our ego instead of from our deepest truth. I've been there – there is nothing that can fill the bottomless pit of needing recognition, acceptance, comfort and fulfilment from an external source. The only real solution is to align with our truth and come from the place of love, self-worth and connection with Source. From that space, we are not driven by these motivators.

READER'S THOUGHT QUEST:
Which of the five motivators, right now, is your biggest motivator?

ACTION SESSION:
Requirements: A journal and a pen

Look at each of the significant moments of your life that you listed above and consider the possibility that your current feelings about them have been influenced by one or more of the five motivators when they took place. List one or more motivators that may have influenced your feelings about each significant moment. (If you were aligned during any of your significant moments, you might observe that you weren't influenced by any of the five motivators.)

For example, you might write:

- I won a writing contest at school when I was twelve and no one in my family attempted to be there when I received the award. (**Motivator: to know who I am matters.**)
- I bought my first car when I was twenty years old after working two jobs and attending college at the same time. (**Motivator: to feel fulfilled.**)

OBSERVATION:
- Did you have any epiphanies when doing this exercise?
- How do you feel now, knowing which motivators influenced your feelings when the events took place? Do you feel the same? Or do you feel differently?
- Do you feel more objective about those moments, or are you still attached to the same emotions?

There are no right or wrong answers. This is simply an observation.

THE TAKE-HOME:
- Perception shapes your world.
- Changing your perception changes your world.

Chapter 8
THE NINE BASE FEARS

Fear is usually the point where you begin a story in your head. The way the story goes depends on your next thought and the thought after that. Every doubt you have is based on some type of fear. These are the nine base fears:

- Fear of rejection
- Fear of discomfort or change
- Fear of standing alone
- Fear of pain
- Fear of being invisible
- Fear of disappointment
- Fear of emptiness
- Fear of the future
- Fear of failure

Like all emotions, fear is an indicator – it helps you recognise what thoughts you are holding onto and how significant they are. The more troubling the thought, the greater your fear reaction. That is powerful because your thoughts create your reality – the way you think about something determines the words you are going to speak and the actions you are going to take.

To understand the symptom, go to the cause. If fear is the symptom, what is the cause?

Distrust of your own worth.

Here's why:

Think about which of the fears above are yours. How many have you experienced?

For each fear, you have woven a story about why your fear is justified and why you shouldn't break through that fear or what the consequences could be. Your story extends the fear – the symptom with an unexplored underlying cause.

Let's explore the cause.

At the beginning of Part 1, I described one of my stories of rejection. I shared about the actions of a national tennis player towards me. Being picked on felt like a manifestation of my fear of rejection. At the basis of me internalising that story was a flawed belief that perpetuated itself throughout my life – "Who I am is wrong." My distrust of my worth increased the strength of the flawed belief every time I perceived someone judging me.

READER'S THOUGHT QUEST:

Which of the fears above have you felt most in your life? What story jumps out at you when you think of such a fear?

ACTION SESSION:

Requirements: A journal and a pen

Write the story with the following points:

- What happened?
- Whose words or actions did you internalise and allow to consume you?
- What were those words and actions?

Now think of someone you love and put them in your shoes in that story. Answer the following questions in your journal, even though the answers may feel obvious:

- Would you want this person you love to internalise the impact of words and actions that did not serve them?
- Would *you* think of them as less worthy because of what was said about or to them?
- What would your advice to them be?

OBSERVATION:

Are you able to realise that the words and actions of any individual come from their own experience of life and possibly from their own flawed belief system based on fear?

THE TAKE-HOME:

The words and actions of said individual cannot be taken as truth. That individual had their own fears at the basis of their own story which influenced their behaviour towards you.

The foundation of what you believed about yourself based on what someone said or did has crumbled. Now what? Where does that leave you? You are at the beginning, aware that your worth has a much deeper meaning.

You are also aware that no matter how anyone behaved towards you or what they thought or said about you, the relationship is between you and you. It's about whether YOU accept their thoughts, words and actions as true and whether you choose to allow the thoughts, words and actions into YOUR story.

Chapter 9
WHY FEAR HAS YOUR BACK DAILY

- Fear tunes you in to the fact that you need to give your BE-ing attention and examine the story you are telling yourself.
- Your thoughts surrounding the fear then determine your words and your actions.
- You can project the outcome and change it – change your thoughts about a topic (UN-tell the story and connect with your worth) and your words and actions will automatically align with your new thoughts.
- You have now empowered yourself because you have the power to rise and change your reality, even if it is in a small way.

When you feel fear rising inside you, check your thoughts, close your eyes, breathe and mentally take a step back.

You are not your thoughts. You can UN-tell the story.

You have the power to collaborate with your thoughts to create a better moment, right here, right now.

READER'S THOUGHT QUEST:
Think about one thing in your life that scares you or causes you stress.

ACTION SESSION:
Requirements: A journal and pen

- Which of the nine base fears relate to this feeling? Write the fear(s) in your journal.
- Write why these fears do NOT have power over you in this moment. Put another way, write a few bullet points about why you are okay – what feels right about your life in this moment? (It can be as basic as the fact that your heart is beating, you are breathing, you have air to breathe and water to drink.)

OBSERVATION:
- How do you feel right now? Do you feel a little better than when you first thought about something that scared you or caused you stress?

THE TAKE-HOME:
- Your perception gives or takes away your power.
- You create your perception, therefore *you have power*.
- You have the power to UN-create fear.

Chapter 10
THE AWAKENING

Everyone has a journey; a moment in time or a life-changing event that leads them to the point of searching. They reach the place where they are ready to find something more – something honest that is beyond the representation of mere words, where they can find the thing itself. I recognised my moment as it happened, then documented it. I knew a significant spiritual and emotional journey had begun. I call that moment my point of awareness.

I dedicate this chapter to you finding and embracing **your** point of awareness. You may identify with the feelings in my snippets of blog entries which I've shared below. I was at my most vulnerable. My words reflected my raw emotions. I'm sharing my words so that you know you're not alone, and that your point of awareness can be the beginning of a significant journey if you allow it to be so.

Reader's thought quest:
Have you experienced a moment of impact that led to your searching for something more?

ACTION SESSION:

Requirements: A journal and a pen

If your answer to the Thought Quest was yes, write, in a sentence or two, the specific event that took place.

Chapter 11
THE SIGNIFICANT MOMENT

I came face-to-face with reality on a sunny Saturday in August when I was standing in the change room of a corsetiere's shop. Like so many women worldwide, I couldn't find a bra that would fit me on the shelf of any mainstream clothing store. Apparently, small built women aren't supposed to have big chests. In South Africa, we have a few corsetieres who specialise in creating custom-made bras for this reason.

About two weeks before said reality-check, I had noticed that my right breast was a little bigger than my left breast. I chose to ignore the situation, deny it or explain it away with anything that sounded mildly plausible when I was forced to look at my breast every morning in the shower. Then came that morning in the change room of the corsetiere's shop – he broke protocol and asked when I had last gone for a mammogram. Even inside that moment, I felt its significance.

Instantly, the energy seemed to drain out of my body and I felt the need for air. *Something must be very wrong if a male corsetiere of all people can notice* – I couldn't silence that thought. I thanked him for his concern and outwardly pulled myself together. On the inside, I was in panic mode! The two-hour drive home seemed like an eternity. I couldn't wait to get to my laptop and start researching the cause of change in breast size. My mind tried on every scenario there could be, including what would make up a horror movie of my life.

We often hear that knowledge is power. But knowledge brings fear. I come from a medical family – my dad was a doctor and my mom is a nurse. I grew up knowing about the possibilities of what could go wrong in the body and what complications could arise. I've been through my sister's more-than-ten-year healing journey, and my dad being seriously ill and crossing over to the Other Side. I didn't know how to stop being scared of whatever was going on in my breast.

I was so panicked that I didn't mention the challenge to anyone except my mom and sister, which was unusual for me. I'm not a private person – I find comfort in sharing with my tribe. The good news about panic is that it doesn't last that long. We humans have the capacity to live with most circumstances by creating a new normal. The not-so-good news is that panic comes in waves, and rarely makes a clean break with the panicker!

READER'S THOUGHT QUEST:
Have you had an awakening from your significant moment? What was your awakening, and what meaning did you give to the event that led to this awakening? Does the event hold a certain emotion?

ACTION SESSION:
Requirements: A journal and a pen

Examine the awakening in *your* life. Write in your journal:

- What do you feel about this event?
- How did you know the moment was significant?
- How has the awakening affected your life?

Chapter 12

THE BIG, SCARY (FILL IN THE BLANK)

Desperation is a powerful motivator. In my quest to make this physical challenge go away, I researched every possible cause; every possible solution. My sister and I were in the home stretch of preparing for our annual girls' empowerment event, *Empowered Girl – Empowered World*. I decided to put the event first. The Sunday night after our event, I phoned a doctor – the first conventional G.P. I'd ever consulted other than my dad. It felt strange to hear the words come out of my mouth: "I think I have a fibroadenoma in my right breast. I did some research and that's what I think it is."

The appointment the next day was stressful. The mammogram and ultrasound results confirmed my Google-researched diagnosis – a benign tumour known as a fibroadenoma. There was a short-lived sigh of relief with that confirmation. I should have been ecstatic, and would have been, except that, because of the large size of the growth, the only solution the doctor recommended was surgery. Knowing the risks of surgery, panic took over again.

Living as healthily as I do, in my mind, there was no reason the fibroadenoma should have been in my breast at all. The cause had to be emotional. I made the unconscious decision to connect with the tumour. The first and most important thing I did was to cut out the white noise from my life and give myself some quiet time every morning and every night.

In the spirit of the adage, *when the student is ready, the teacher will appear*, I developed a sense of clarity the moment I was open to learn, think differently and feel differently. I realised this fibroadenoma was here for a purpose – instead of wanting it to go away, it was time to question why it was here. So I did something crazy by most people's standards. I wrote letters to the tumour:

Dear fibroadenoma,

What are you here to teach me? I wanted you gone ever since I discovered you. I know I created you, and I'm working on not blaming myself for it… I think I attracted you into my experience because I needed to learn something or embark on this journey. So I silently accept your lesson whenever it comes and whatever it is. I'm still scared – of you, of my own emotions, of where this path will lead.

Dear fibroadenoma,

I wish you peace and love, and I want to say gratitude – maybe later I'll find it within me to do that.

Dear fibroadenoma,

I can't decide how I feel about you. Yesterday I wished you peace and love. Today I'm ambivalent. Will I ever not fear you or what you can do? But that doesn't mean I'm not positive, because, I am! I realise that life is still exciting and you aren't the worst thing that happened to me. I'll be okay!

Why does it take what seems to be a potential disaster to jar one into getting back on track with one's purpose? Is pain necessary to help us learn a lesson or to spur us on to action? I don't believe so, but it was the path that I had chosen, albeit unconsciously. My learning curve began fast and furiously.

READER'S THOUGHT QUEST:
What is the title of YOUR chapter? Fill in the blank with whatever you named the challenge. The Big Scary_____. My title was, The Big Scary Fibroadenoma.

ACTION SESSION:
Requirements: A journal and a pen

- Now that you've filled in the blank, what inspired action steps will you take to deal with the challenge. List them.
- In what ways can you cut out the white noise from your life? List them.
- What is a good time every day to give yourself some quiet time? Write this in your journal.
- Write a letter to the challenge and tell it how you feel.

Chapter 13
LET THE JOURNEY UN-FOLD

I realised that for the first time in a long while; I was getting back on track spiritually. I hadn't felt the joy and sureness of being connected to Source and hadn't made time to acknowledge or feel this Divine Connection. For your purpose, define this connection in any way that resonates with you – call it God, Source, Universe, Divine Presence, Higher Self, your centre, or your heart.

I had felt disconnected and lost without a sense of this connection. The realisation hit that I needed to heal my BE-ing. I felt broken and damaged, experiencing the sensation that I was in some sort of bubble of my creation that didn't give me the capacity to feel anything deeply. Perhaps I had unconsciously created a protection mechanism to shield me from pain.

The fibroadenoma in my breast had a greater purpose than I could comprehend when it made its presence known in my body. Its presence was not of significance, but it was the impetus for a journey within to know my connection with Source again.

READER'S THOUGHT QUEST:

Do you feel connected with YOU? Has your challenge brought you a realisation?

ACTION SESSION:

Requirements: A journal and a pen

Write the realisation or epiphany you've had, if you've had one.

Chapter 14
GRATITUDE

I had arranged the surgery to remove the fibroadenoma. I knew it was not some sort of quick fix or an end to this journey. It was a stepping stone. I had finally found gratitude for this unwelcome growth invading my body. As much as the thought of surgery was stressful, it could be a spiritual experience if I allowed this.

READER'S THOUGHT QUEST:
Have you experienced gratitude for your challenge?

ACTION SESSION:
Requirements: A journal and a pen

If your answer to the Thought Quest was yes, list what you are grateful for. This exercise is not about *thinking* – it is about *feeling* gratitude. If you don't feel it, don't write it down.

Chapter 15
LETTING GO

The day before the surgery, I met my doctor, a plastic and reconstructive surgeon. He was everything I'd hoped for – kind, compassionate, willing to answer every question, and had that quiet confidence that all people who are great at their professions seem to exude. I instantly felt relieved, knowing I was in good hands.

The day of the excision was a trail mix of emotion, disconnected thoughts and stress! I met my anaesthetist, who was waiting for me when I walked in five minutes late. He was a gentle, kind, patient man who explained exactly what would happen when he anaesthetised me. Surgery was becoming a reality. As a patient, I had to set the tone, and I had a choice in doing that: either panic and have the doctors calm me down, or silently let them know I believed in their abilities and knew the surgery was going to go well. I chose the latter. Choosing the significance of this event was up to me, and I wanted it to be a part of my spiritual healing. For weeks I'd been agonising over this fibroadenoma, which, along with reawakening my spiritual awareness, had dominated most of my thoughts and feelings. My surgeon had agreed to take a picture of the big, scary fibroadenoma. I needed to see it.

The last thing I remember is having a conversation with the anaesthetist and nurse and being asked to count backwards from ten...

Letting go is allowing ego to dissolve in the moment; BE-ing in the space of deepest truth and trusting Source within. It is aligning with my Divinity for my Divine Purpose.

READER'S THOUGHT QUEST:
Have you chosen the significance of your experience? Have you empowered yourself through your choices?

ACTION SESSION:
Requirements: A journal and a pen

Write the significance of your experience. If you haven't reached the point of giving your experience meaning, write three empowering choices you made during your experience, or three empowering choices you are making now to collaborate with the experience.

Chapter 16
THE RIDE OF YOUR LIFE

To enjoy riding a bike you need to find balance, otherwise it's a painful and unpleasant experience. Once you have confidence that you can find your balance, there is that carefree feeling of joy and freedom and having the wind in your hair – you feel invincible!

This gift, the big, scary fibroadenoma, the starting point of my journey, taught me to trust that the Universe will catch me when I feel off-centre; that I will never fall. Coming back to centre is a given. Why has it taken me so long to know this and feel it? Did I never feel safe in this lifetime? I don't know the answers to these questions. I know it is time to make a change.

The concept of change sounds good – a clean slate; a big and exciting new adventure; the road to happiness. But change isn't glitzy and glamorous. It is doing something small consistently, when such an action, in the moment, doesn't seem to make a difference. No one knows about your small, consistent steps. There is no cheering or epic music playing in the background. You get to decide what value the change will hold for you and its purpose in your life. The decision is private, and you will not receive any external accolades for your choices. Will you still take those incremental steps to change?

READER'S THOUGHT QUEST:
Have you decided to create change in your life? What is the value of the change and its purpose for you?

ACTION SESSION:
Requirements: A journal and a pen

If you've decided that your challenge will be a catalyst for change, what is the change you've decided to make? Why? Write about the change without analysing your thoughts and clouding your vision. Write purely from the heart.

Chapter 17
YOU DON'T SCARE ME ANYMORE

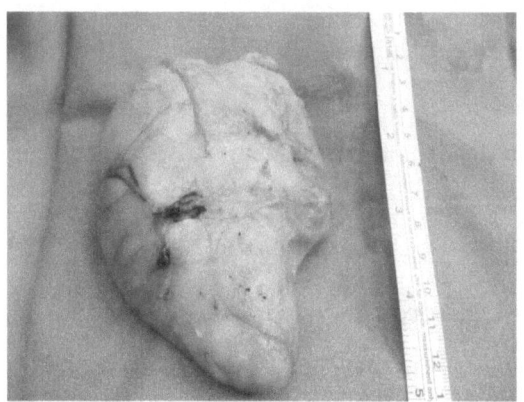

Dear Fibroadenoma,

You don't scare me anymore…well, to be honest, looking at this picture does scare me a little. I can't pin down a specific emotion, but I certainly feel a lot when I look at the picture and think that something so big was growing in my body; that every negative emotion, thought and word I had kept inside without releasing, could manifest into something so physical!

Yet, I am thankful for this physical indicator of my life going so far off track. I have never felt so scared and out of control before. The resulting journey of healing has given me unequalled moments of clarity and epiphanies I wouldn't otherwise have had. My greatest fear has become my greatest blessing.

I can now feel a sense of peace and joy that I wasn't able to experience before. I have you to thank for that. So, like I said, you don't scare me much anymore and you have proven to be an incredible teacher!

Having written that letter, I'm staring the fibroadenoma in the face and thinking about the incredible lessons that came from the experience:

1. I *can* trust the Universe to support me.
2. It's okay to let go and allow my loved ones to take care of me physically and emotionally. It is okay to lean on them for support.
3. I can choose the meaning I give to any experience.
4. Divine Guidance is always available – it is my choice to seek it.
5. I have learned to breathe deeply with ease.
6. Having fun every day is a valuable part of life that nourishes my soul.
7. I need to ask for support when I need it, and there will always be support available.
8. Staring fear in the face and embracing it is an important part of healing to my next level.
9. Part of my life's purpose is to experience joy.
10. Taking time for ME needs to be a priority, not a luxury.

11. It *is* possible to have twelve worry-free days!
12. Physical symptoms are indicators of one's emotions, which in turn are an indicator of one's vibration.
13. Speaking my truth and living it is the way I choose to BE.
14. It is okay to feel every experience and emotion deeply. I will never again shut myself off to feeling things! Processing my emotions is essential.
15. Every thought counts. I now examine my thoughts and learn the truth about why they're there.
16. Asking WHY is essential to living my deepest truth.
17. It is possible to do nothing at all and give my body a complete rest.
18. No matter what, I always have the ability to come back to centre.
19. Synchronicities mean something. Nothing in life is a random coincidence.
20. Trusting in Perfect Divine Timing is the road to inner peace.
21. It is okay to admit how scared I am.
22. Accepting and appreciating the gift of the challenge is where healing begins.
23. Life is good.
24. I love my body, just as it is, with my battle scars which tell a story of what I've overcome – that includes my breast!
25. I will be okay no matter what (and the same goes for you).

26. I am important. My feelings are important. Speaking my truth is important. You are important. Your feelings are important. Speaking your truth is important.

27. This journey continues – the journey of loving, living, laughing, learning and chocolate (chocolate makes the world a better place).

If you're wondering, the measuring tape next to the fibroadenoma in the picture is an accurate representation – it *was* that big (105 x 70 x 52 mm) and it weighed 139.5g!

READER'S THOUGHT QUEST:
Do you feel differently about your challenge than the first time you wrote a letter to it? What lessons came from your experience?

ACTION SESSION:
Requirements: A journal and a pen

Write a letter to your challenge, then read it. Do you feel you're communicating with your challenge differently? Write the lessons from your experience and read them. How do you feel about your challenge now?

Chapter 18
MOVING OUT OF NO MAN'S LAND

It seems I'm grieving. Not for anyone. I'm grieving for a life a million years ago that seemed to resemble some sort of normal. Before being caregiver when my sister was on her healing journey; before my dad crossed over; before gluten-free, dairy-free whole foods.

When you long for aspects of a life you had in the past, you remember that you were a different person back then. Life experiences that present themselves as challenges bring a healthy dose of personal growth with them and you evolve. In the now, it is hard to imagine being the person you were back then. So you realise that you're in no man's land – longing for the simplicity of the past, while wanting to BE who you are right now.

It's time for me to move out of no man's land and find a new normal. What is normal? Who defines it? It's an overdone word with no clear meaning, except in the eyes of the person searching for it. Along with the excision of the fibroadenoma and spending the night in hospital, I was gifted with some space to think, feel, reframe, and come up with my definition of normal. After all the lessons and epiphanies, there was an incubation period– a time when the newly formed realisations gradually became integrated with my BE-ing. I got to know *me* as the realisations slowly became a part of me. I got to UN-define the previous version of me.

READER'S THOUGHT QUEST:
- What realisations (if any) have you had about the story of your life as a whole?
- What realisations (if any) have you had about your new normal or the new chapter of your life that began with your point of awareness?
- Do you feel you're willing and ready to incorporate your point of awareness with your truth?

ACTION SESSION:
Requirements: A journal and a pen (or your laptop, an audio recording or video recording app, or a sketch book)

Start keeping a journal. The word "journal" is used broadly. If writing isn't your thing, use audio or video recording, drawing or collaging as a means of expression. Journal on days when you have strong thoughts, realisations and emotions, whether you perceive them as positive or negative. Allow them to become your teachers and give value to your now.

OBSERVATION:
- This exercise will require you to be conscious of how you're feeling and what you're thinking each day.
- Take note of your thoughts and emotions when you wake up and again when you go to bed.

THE TAKE-HOME:

Living your truth is about aligning the story of your life with the truth of your soul. Your thoughts and emotions are indicators of your energy at any specific moment; your energy will shape your world and how you relate to it.

Part 3: JOURNEY OF SEEKING

The adventure of seeking begins right here, right now. What does adventure have to do with your spiritual journey and evolution? EVERYTHING. Do you remember that feeling as a child when possibility and adventure was so exciting? Do you remember reading a book or watching a movie about finding treasure and following maps? Do you remember the excitement in replacing the hero with YOU in the adventure? What would you do? Where would you go? What treasures could you UN-earth in your own adventure?

The feeling of that childhood excitement bubbling out of you is what you need in order to be in alignment with the deepest part of you where there is no fear, insecurity, ego or limit. It starts with recreating the feeling of adventurous exploration, and UN-limiting yourself in every way.

This is YOUR adventure. BE with it!

> **Important definitions:**
>
> **Point A:** The point of awareness; your starting point; where you are now (a point that has no bearing on your happiness or your reaching of Point B).
>
> **Point B:** Your dream or vision of where you want to BE; the place of alignment in mind-body-spirit (there will be many Point B's throughout your life).

Chapter 19
YOUR QUEST

Where are you?

You're starting at Point A, and your point B is where you want to BE. It's important to know the truth of where you are in order to navigate to your Point B.

You got here through your own thoughts, beliefs, words, actions and interactions, as well as the importance you placed on the thoughts, beliefs, words, actions and interactions of those who mean something to you.

Would that be an accurate statement?

More exploration will reveal your exact coordinates. The questions below will help. Don't think too much about your answers – read each question and follow your first instinct, since that is your truth.

- Do you trust life right now?

- Do you feel supported by life right now ('supported' according to your own definition)?
- Do you feel you are capable of birthing your desires into your reality?
- Do you feel you are successful (according to your definition of success)?
- When last did you do something kind and loving for yourself?
- Do you feel good about where you are in your life right now?
- Who are the five people you spend the most time with?
- Do you feel that these five people support you (according to your own definition of support)?
- Do you feel as though you have an opportunity to get to your Point B?
- Do you know what your Point B is?
- Do you get up hopeful each day?
- Do you feel free to BE who you are?
- When in your life have you felt happy and fulfilled (if you can recall such a time, write it down)?
- Have you ever stopped living your life in the way you wanted to live it? If so, when?

Your answers are not right or wrong. They simply are, and you need no validation from anyone else to justify them. It's okay if you don't have clear-cut answers to the above questions. Your answers or lack of answers indicate the coordinates that describe your Point A to you. Take a minute – read through them. Process them. They don't have any hold on your life. They are not a sign of who you are or where you are going – it is your choices from here on that determine your path.

Knowing your coordinates, it is possible to map out your route to Point B. Examine your map. You are here, and the heavy backpack you're carrying is your story as you know it. On your journey, you'll unpack that backpack, let go of what isn't yours and continue with only your truth. It is easier to travel light, and you'll have the confidence to do it.

Are you ready?

Are you ready to embark on the greatest adventure in this lifetime – the quest to live your truth without limits and get to your Point B?

What does 'ready' mean to you?

When you lie in bed at night, do you hear your heart whisper that it longs for more? Perhaps you're searching for something that you can't quite put your finger on, and it isn't about anything external – it is the search for YOU.

What are the symptoms of your searching, of your being ready to be a Truth-Walker? Do you feel an emptiness when you're alone because it seems something is missing? Maybe you're so restless that you want to shatter the walls of your self-imposed limits with your bare hands, scream with raw emotion and run free wherever the path leads. Or is there a nagging feeling within that you are here to make a difference in the world, and your frustration is in not knowing how?

It is from this place that you probably made the unconscious decision to take a stand for the truth of who you are inside. Your 'why' has become strong enough for you to rise up, UN-Become who you are not, and own your life.

Taking ownership of your life is not about possession – it is BE-ing in co-creation with Source (call it heart, Divinity, God within, Higher Self or whatever feels right for you) and living out your deepest truth in, with and from freedom. Your journey begins here, at your Point A, the point of awareness.

What is your quest?

Before you take your first step, think about the purpose of your quest.

As a Truth-Walker, you are a warrior of sorts. I'm going to UN-define the image that conjures up conflict, fighting against others, winning and losing.

You are a 'warrior' when you have the courage to:

- Accept and love yourself as you are.
- Allow your inner strength to shine through to your external BE-ing and to your every thought, word and action.
- Open yourself to growth and evolution, healing to your next level.
- Commune with the biosphere and geosphere of Mother Earth, knowing that all BE-ings are interconnected and the evolution of one becomes the evolution of all.

In other words, in your unconditional love for who you are, you, as warrior, are ready to rise, BE your Light and honour your calling in this lifetime. As you nourish your own BE-ing, you automatically contribute to nourishing your world. You're on a quest to your Point B. There will be many such quests in your life.

What will you pack?

To know what to pack, consider the nature of the terrain. There is no clear path leading you in a well-defined direction and no markers to signify the completion of your first step (or any step after that). The trail of your deepest truth is yours to blaze.

So, dear Warrior, pack lightly and thoughtfully. Here is a list of the essentials:

- Your map – the tangible steps you can take to live your deepest truth.
- Your Light within – a means to banish darkness and demons such as ego and fear.
- Your voice – your multi-faceted instrument to navigate rough terrain.*

*A note about the voice: This instrument takes many forms. It is in the quiet nudge of intuition, the emotions that rise within, your action or lack of action, and your physical voice. Your voice expresses your truth, indicates where you are, and is the way-shower for change; it is your Innate Wisdom.

You have probably packed many unnecessary items in your backpack, such as your story and your preconceived ideas. That's okay. Know that during your journey, you will let go of items that may have seemed essential when you started out. This process is an integral part of your quest.

What do you need to know?

Dear Truth-Walker, dear brave warrior –

Before you take your first steps, you may have questions. The answers will appear when the time is right. There is one question that can be answered before you begin: where does the warrior find the strength to take a stand for self? That strength has always lived in the deepest recesses of your BE-ing. In the decision to BE a warrior, you will embrace that part of you.

Your strength will allow you to love and accept yourself unconditionally. It will give you the courage to step out and course-correct if necessary, knowing that you have the capacity to get to Point B. Courage will allow you to answer the call to BE the change in your world.

This journey requires two types of actions from you:

1. Take a stand for who you are by giving yourself the physical, spiritual, emotional and psychological nourishment to reach your highest potential – as you do so, you will rise to become the personification of your truth.
2. BE the guardian of what you allow into your mind so that you are in alignment with the truth of your BE-ing.

The lay of the land

Have you looked out in the distance to see what lies beyond Point A? There seems to be some rough terrain out there. Are you daunted by the prospect of navigating your way through it? Know that you have what you need to complete your quest and your point B is reachable.

The terrain you're looking at goes by another name – *change!* Hiking your way through doesn't have to be hard. Those steep, menacing-looking hills in the distance are not as intimidating as they seem – you're seeing them through an illusion known to you as *fear.*

Chapter 20
THE JOURNEY BEGINS

Navigating the terrain

How you navigate the terrain of *change* is your call. You define it and you give it value. The terrain of *change* has the potential to be a catalyst for a renewed zest for life, bringing you closer to Point B.

How to create forward momentum to navigate *change:*

Find a powerful reason to continue forward – one that overcomes any negative perceptions you have about yourself or your capabilities.

1. Be focused on your Point B.
2. Have a game plan of Inspired action steps daily to get to Point B.
3. Have navigation tools (e.g. books, audio recordings, meditations, videos, a coach, stress-relieving activities, like-minded cheerleaders) on hand when the path before you seems rough.
4. Commit to completing your Inspired action plan for the day – make it a part of your daily life.

5. Continue to step forward and take action according to your plan.

6. Find the fun in your action steps and relish the momentum you create.

7. Celebrate your wins with gusto!

Your map to navigate *change:*

1. Cut out the white noise from your life – give yourself some quiet time for a few minutes every morning and every night to *feel* your emotions. What are your emotions? What do you feel physically when you connect with your emotions? It takes courage to be alone with yourself and to feel things you may not be comfortable feeling, but it is the first step to freeing yourself so that you can move forward.

2. Be open to learn that which your heart is yearning for. Give your emotions the respect they deserve and allow the time and space for them to tell you what they need you to know. Emotions are a powerful indicator.

3. Recognise that there is an unspoken truth within you and there is a purpose in all things and in every situation.

4. Connect with those who will support you on your journey of truth. Mentors and teachers are important at this time. If you can't connect with them on a personal level, call in to their radio shows to get some insight, email them, listen to their audio programs and read their books (whichever option is applicable). If you're not sure who your mentor is, take notice of what *you* feel you need in order to feel better. Then find a way to connect with someone who is an expert in helping

you with what you need to feel better. Be open, listen and be teachable.

5. Write a letter to the challenge when you hit rough terrain. Tell the challenge your feelings, and why you're sad, scared, angry or frustrated. Put every feeling you have into this letter. Write a letter to the challenge the next day, and the following day, and every day after that, until you can find some peace in the communication. That's the point of breaking through. Stop writing when you find gratitude in your heart for some aspect of the challenge. This is how I approached my fibroadenoma (see *Part 2: Awareness*) and it worked. It's also therapeutic to read the letters after you have` found gratitude for the challenge.

6. Give it time; allow the journey to UN-fold.

The obstructions

As a warrior, sometimes your external BE-ing feels weary and the vision of your path is unclear because of what you perceive as an obstruction. Seeing obstructions for what they are, enables you to see the solutions available to you.

a. *Comfort zone* – a deceptively feel-good obstruction that may lead to self-imposed paralysis at any stage of your journey. For this reason, it is the most dangerous obstacle. The secret to overcoming it is in recognising that its comfort can keep you from BE-ing your highest potential.

b. *White noise* – the words and actions of fellow BE-ings who cross a warrior's path. Often, these individuals have chosen not to walk the path of the Truth-Walker. The distraction of their footprints may cause detours, re-routes or temporary amnesia about the nature and location of your Point B. White noise may appear in your perception as judgement towards you, friendly advice or ego-filled statements, as well as well-meaning invitations to partake in activities that dim your light or distract you from your quest. Recognise the distractions and focus on your Point B.

c. *Ego* – a condition affecting a warrior's judgement, caused by forgetting the connection with Source (or however you define this connection: heart, your Centre, God within, Higher Self) that is always available. Ego may influence a warrior to act in a way that is out of alignment with their deepest truth or to perceive imaginary obstacles as real.

d. *Insecurity* – a condition that slowly depletes a warrior's energy and perception of their own power, leading the warrior to believe that they have fallen into a black pit where no light is present and no help is available.

e. *Fear* – An ego-inspired illusion of steep hills and rocky ground that may lead to a severe lack of action. It masquerades in many forms (see the Nine Base Fears in *Part 2: Awareness*)

f. *Failure* – The false perception that there is a darkness so black that even thinking about its presence causes extreme exhaustion and discouragement. Failure is often accompanied by white noise.

Failure is a shadow created when you have dimmed your light and ego sets in. Fear is the younger sibling of failure – an imaginary shadow made real by ego-inspired thoughts.

Insecurity, fear and failure fall under the umbrella of ego and have the same cause – distrust of your own worth (See *Part 2: Awareness*).

Chapter 21
ACCESSING YOUR TRAVEL GEAR

Instructions for using your Light

In order for your greatest tool, your Light, to remain at its brightest, you must nourish it through self-love. Use your Light to view your map more easily and to see the obstacles in front of you for what they are – illusions created by your perception of darkness. You will discover that the reach of your Light has no limits, and your Point B will become visible in the distance.

Instructions for using your voice

Your voice may not seem powerful at first. For many Truth-Walkers, this instrument seems useless on first inspection. It needs to be activated since it may have been negatively affected through past experiences or muted by white noise.

Signs that your voice is not activated or may have been muted:

- You haven't felt its power, nor have you given credence to this instrument.
- You feel that you want to scream with all the rage, passion, pain and power within you but you're afraid that no sound would come out if you tried.
- Your voice no longer acts as the connection between your truth and your interactions with your world.

In this moment of deafening silence, you have the power to reconnect with this part of you that you think you have lost. You never really lost it, but you stopped treating it as though it mattered. It does. It is an integral part of who you are, and YOU matter. Your voice matters.

What to do to reactivate your voice if it has been muted:

- Breathe deeply, be with your Centre (Source within) and recognise the connection of your Centre to your voice.
- Find the time to BE in stillness regularly and listen to your emotions and intuition – the quiet whispers of your voice.
- Allow your voice to surface fully in its own time.
- The more you use this instrument of truth, the more powerful it will become.

The functions and power of your voice as a Truth-Walker

- It makes itself known through powerful feelings within.
- It doesn't come in neatly packaged words or controlled actions. It is not contrived – it is a natural release of emotion and thought that asks to be heard.

- It tells you when you are afraid, asks you to recognise your fear, and invites you to look deeper and listen.
- It peels away the layers of your anger and exposes your insecurities.
- It cuts through your emotions and shows you the bedrock of pain at their root.
- Your voice expresses your Light.
- It gives meaning to your every feeling, thought, word, and action if you allow it to do so.
- Your voice is integral in the UN-Becoming of who you are not.

In your every interaction, the world asks what you are saying. When your voice connects with your deepest truth, your message to the world rings out as authentic, purposeful, and credible.

Chapter 22
YOUR CHOICE

What do you do when you feel a situation cannot be changed; when the lay of the land seems to make your path inaccessible? As warrior, you take a step back to observe the status quo from different angles. Then you change the most important thing – your perspective; your story. You pivot.

Transformation within inspires transformation externally.

Analyse your story:

- What story have you been telling yourself about who you are and your situation?
- Does your story feel accurate?
- Does your story cause you to feel pain, anger, sadness or regret?
- Is it empowering?
- Does it enable you to move forward?

If your story does not reflect your truth that you are strong, capable and courageous, finding a navigable path must entail UN-telling your story so that your path to Point B takes its cue from your truth. Use the guidance in *Part 2: Awareness* to UN-tell your story.

The facts of a situation are not the same as the truth of a situation.

You are faced with a choice, dear Warrior. The significance of your journey, and whether you value the idea of taking such a journey, is chosen solely by you. Will you continue even when obstacles seem insurmountable and your path seems barricaded to you?

Your journey allows you to form your own definition of YOU, your life, your importance in your life, and your success. Your Point B is in the distance—it is your choice to get there, or to adhere to the status quo.

Chapter 23
CLAIMING SOVEREIGNTY

Dropping the cloak and the mask

It is time. You drop the backpack beside you and begin unpacking it. Every sentimental item that has been adding to your load gets taken out. The Truth-Walker does not need it. You feel freer and lighter. Your burdens are less. Finally, you stand up, realising that you do not need the backpack. Your cloak falls from your back – one of the last items that has hidden your BE-ing.

You kneel at the edge of the stream, stare at your reflection and wash the warrior's paint off your face. A warrior does not need paint. You scoop some water into your mouth. For the first time, you taste its goodness and feel its nourishment seep into your BE-ing.

Reclaiming your space of power

Your quest will lead you to a beautiful, sunlit space where you feel an inner peace. You will recognise it through feeling its energy and noticing the following shifts within:

- You feel alignment with Source (Divine Connection, heart, your Centre, God within, Higher Self).
- Your Light is at its brightest and you can cast out the white noise around you easily.
- You notice yourself suspending your previous fear and resistance.
- You easily silence your ego.
- Your truth makes itself known when you spend time in meditation.

You are now in the best place to BE your greatest potential and map out your way to Point B.

You lack nothing, Truth-Walker! That deepest part of you knows no fear or insecurity, and does not perceive limits or failure. You have stepped into BE-ing in external thought, word and action, who you are within.

Taking stock of where you are

Examine your map, Truth-Walker. Where are you?

Change, the sometimes intimidating terrain that you've been navigating, has sparked the process of examining the 'why', 'how' and 'what next' of your life.

By now, you will have observed:

- You are conscious of your intention in every thought, word, and action.
- You ask yourself what your truth is and whether you're coming from Source within, or from your ego.

- You think about the purpose of your words and actions as you interact with yourself and your fellow BE-ings.

Your Inner Guidance and connection to your deepest truth, provide direction to take your next step.

Stepping forward

Your journey to this point opened you, and you came face-to-face with yourself. In your nakedness, you were vulnerable. Yet, it is from this vulnerability that you found your power. The essence of who you are emerged externally – powerful, purposeful and profound.

This shift in your BE-ing shows in your external appearance and the way you carry yourself.

What are your objectives in your interactions as a Truth-Walker?

- Silence your ego and come from the place of your deepest truth.
- Communicate your truth in a way that it can be received – speak in a way that the receiver can best understand your message, while BE-ing in integrity with your truth.
- BE independent of the receiver's thoughts of you.
- BE independent of who walks the path with you or how they choose to navigate it.

Chapter 24
APPLYING THE SHIFT WITHIN

The big question

Do you feel worthy of who you are inside?

This question will surface in different forms, and many times, as you journey through the different levels of your evolution as a Truth-Walker. You will have a real and lasting impact as a Truth-Walker in those moments when you can answer, "Yes."

The epiphany

You scan the map before you. You are at a point of epiphany. Breathless, you climb onto the highest nearby rock and scan your surroundings – uneven terrain, steep hills, cliffs, thorn bushes, the wind biting at your back, and the sun licking your aching calves. Look at all that you have overcome, Truth-Walker – it is as though the land has surrendered to you. Something has dawned on you. Before this moment, you thought you were navigating the change and now you realise that you ARE the change. It is about YOU – your path, your definition, your terms.

You are the change within and with-out. You have the power. You ARE the power.

Who will you BE?

You are well-practised in shining your Light brightly, Truth-Walker. You have expanded its reach to where you can see your Point B clearly. You can also see Point A in the distance if you turn around. Now, more than ever, you want to keep your focus. There are a few things you are nostalgic about when you view Point A from your present vantage point. But you know with certainty that you want to move forward. Sometimes you are afraid that you will falter to the temptations and obstacles along your path. Then you close your eyes and remember who you are – the Warrior, the Truth-Walker.

At times on your journey, you may be tempted to allow your fears of feeling incapable, unworthy, misunderstood or alone in the storm, to govern your quest. What the storm is asking you is, "Who are you in this moment?"

You get to decide what your answer will be.

Interacting with your world

As much as we interact with our external world, how we feel about the interaction is a reflection of our relationship with self. How do you, as Truth-Walker, respond to your perception of your own failure regarding interactions with your external world?

- Remind yourself that failure does not exist, except in your mind.
- Embrace your growth to this point in your journey.
- Treat yourself as lovingly and kindly as you would treat anyone else. Do not let your perceived failure define you or hold you back.
- Remind yourself of your worthiness. Source within revels in the wholeness that is YOU. You ARE worthy – it's a matter of recognising your worth.

How to handle what you perceive as judgement from your world

- Know that judgement always comes from self – it is a choice to receive said judgement.
- Know that judgement is universal – all of us have been judge and judged.
- Know that judgement does not define you. Only YOU define you.
- Respect the right of your fellow BE-ings to hold a different opinion to yours.
- Respect yourself by not allowing into your mind the thoughts that do not serve you.

Chapter 25
THE ESSENCE OF THE SEEKING

A better world

Look up at the blue of the sky, dear Truth-Walker. You could get lost in it. But what is even more mesmerising is the beauty of the world you are standing in. You care deeply for this world. Now that you recognise and feel filled with the gifts of the entire Universe, you have the power to use your Light and your voice to create a better world.

Our commonalities

Each of us, as Truth-Walker, creates a shift within and, through this shift, inspires evolution in our external environment. Therefore, each of us produces a ripple effect by means of the journey of our existence.

Our commonalities on a practical level:

- We each seek a Point B.

- We are each able to choose who to BE through our individual experiences.
- We each create a unique ripple effect in our world through our thoughts, words and actions.

We recognise that there can be no ONE universal truth that can guide ALL of us or that we can all 'fit' into. We accept and love a world where every BE-ing can live out their Divine truth in, with and from freedom. We are each part of the greater whole; how we choose to connect with the whole and how we observe that connection is individual.

Through these commonalities, we have the power to create a better world together. As Truth-Walkers, we get to protect:

- The right of every BE-ing on Mother Earth to live out their individuality.
- The right of every BE-ing on Mother Earth to be a contributor to their world in their own way.
- The right of every BE-ing on Mother Earth to embark on the quest to live their truth in, with and from freedom.

The dream

Dear Truth-Walker; dear Brave Warrior –

You have in your hands the map to get from your Point A to Point B. It has no power. You are the one with the power.

Close your eyes. Imagine being able to wake up tomorrow morning and live your truth. You embrace all facets of who you are, you love, you laugh, you learn. You live your life to the fullest, according to your own definition of what that means. You create your world as you wish to see it.

You shouldn't have to close your eyes to live a life like that. Right now, you have a choice. What you do next will make the difference.

You've seen yourself as you are; you've seen the truth of your essence. Let me ask you this: what is it that you dream of? What is it that sparks the flicker of hope beyond the horizon that only your eyes can see?

Are you afraid of it? Are you afraid to give voice to the truth of your dreams? It doesn't matter that they are way out there, far beyond the land you are accustomed to walking. Your dreams lie out on that hallowed ground that only **your** brave thoughts have touched. Will you claim that hallowed ground as your future?

Your dream has risen from deep within you and seeped into your consciousness because it chose you. And you, as the chosen one, have the privilege and honour of walking towards it, step by step. You will get there as long as you remember who you are. You are the keeper of the Light.

Part 4:
UN-BECOMING

Chapter 26
THE FULLNESS OF BE-ING EMPTY

There's a question many of us struggle with when getting to our next level. Who will I be if I am empty? If my life is not filled with the chaos of the ego and the white noise of daily life, what will my life mean? If I let go of all that does not serve me, will there be anything left, or will I be an empty vessel that is hollow?

These are superficial questions masking the genuine concern: Am I worthy enough to accept my BE-ing in its nakedness and its wholeness? There is no question of your worthiness – of course you are worthy! But your question relates to whether you *feel* you are worthy. When there is chaos and white noise, we don't have to face the fear of feeling unworthy – there is no time and space to have the courage to accept ourselves fully and look ourselves in the eyes.

If you don't feel worthy of the gift of who you are, your defence mechanism kicks in – busyness, procrastination and the resulting overwhelm.

When you cut out the white noise and create space for breath and breathing, thoughts, words, emotions and inspired actions, you begin to honour your mind, body and spirit.

UN-Becoming is the act of creating that space until you feel the Light of your BE-ing shining through your thoughts, words, and actions.

What does this mean for you on a personal and daily level? The space increases your awareness of your Light. The fullness of who we are is not created by society's structures that we live by. These structures have changed through different eras. In times past, a man's value was judged by how many cattle he owned. Similarly, the norm was that a woman's value was determined by her marital status or the career path of her husband. In our world today, these constructs still exist in various forms.

If your worth is based on external circumstances, then your worth is always changing, like fluctuations in the stock market. You are not a commodity to be bought and sold, sometimes valuable and sometimes valueless. You are a powerful BE-ing of Light.

You are beyond change and beyond the illusions created by culture or society. Money, achievements or marital status do not determine your worth. Your worth is also not determined by opinions, expectations, circumstances, words, thoughts and actions that don't align with who you are. These external constructs do not define you.

It is time to question constructs and rules that don't feel aligned with your deepest truth. Question their meaning and the agendas attached to them. There will always be constructs and there will always be agendas – the only thing that matters is whether your perception of them is aligned with your deepest truth. If you feel misaligned, your greatest act of service and leadership is to raise your vibration to alignment. Your vibration is the energy you bring to the table – to your own BE-ing and your fellow BE-ings.

Every external construct in our world may crumble to dust, but your energy remains beyond the external. Energy cannot be created or destroyed; it can only be transformed from one form to another. Therefore, your energy is the real YOU. Every external condition you perceive is just a reflection of your vibration in that moment. The power to create change within and in the greater world, is in the energy you bring to the table.

Chapter 27
UN-BECOMING DEFINED

Many people are cloaked by the trappings determined by society – the constraints of things like religious practices passed down from parents, cultural norms they feel obligated to follow, clothes they feel forced to wear, names they feel obligated to call their children, languages they feel forced to express themselves in, roles they feel they must play. These trappings are not who they are or how they see themselves. When they have the tools to UN-Become who they are not, and they use these tools, what remains is the truth of who they are in all its nakedness and vulnerability. Their truth becomes the starting point of how they live their lives – there is a shift in how they see their world, and a plethora of possibilities open up. This is the beginning of their journey to self-love and self-worth.

Let's go to the premise of this journey to UN-Become who you are not. We are not talking about a transformation here or a revolution, but about UN-earthing the truth of your BE-ing. The UN-earthing of truth is not a transformational process or a bad habit that is broken – it is the peeling away of layers of conditioning and indoctrination to reveal what was always there. Like Glinda said to Dorothy in The Wizard of Oz, "Everything you were looking for was right there with you all along."

The science behind UN-Becoming

We define corrosion as the destructive and unintentional degradation of a material caused by its environment. Now let's look at a pair of stainless-steel scissors that gets corroded by the elements. While the corrosion is a natural process, and the scissors interacting with its environment is inevitable, the corrosion can still cause the scissors to be damaged, such that the scissors may become weak or lose its function (its sole purpose) to cut items. We dip the scissors in vinegar to dissolve the rust, and the scissors returns to its true nature and is reminded of its purpose and ability. We have helped the scissors to UN-Become what it is not.

Another example is a parasitic plant which has lived on a host plant for so long that the host plant doesn't even realise the parasite is there. Through its haustoria (modified roots), the parasite has attached itself to the xylem or phloem (conductive system) of the host plant, extracting water and nutrients from the host. The host plant experiences weakness, but perhaps doesn't realise the full extent to which it is being damaged. When we help to extricate the parasite from the host plant, we are helping the host plant to UN-Become what it is not, bringing its true nature into focus. The plant can now BE its true potential – it couldn't do this if it didn't UN-Become what it is not.

Chapter 28
RED ZONE OR REBIRTH ZONE

How do we begin the journey to live in our deepest truth? First, we recognise our intention to UN-Become who we are not. In doing so, we are opening up the possibility of our potential, even if we do not believe in our potential yet.

Next, we need to know where we are, in order to map our way to where we are going. Are you in the Red Zone or the Rebirth Zone?

- The Red Zone and the Rebirth Zone are like the two opposite poles of a magnet.
- The **Rebirth Zone** is where we want to be. It is our Point B. When we are in the Rebirth Zone, we are in our zone of creativity, and we feel connected to who we are at the deepest level. We have UN-Become who we are not – our thoughts, words and actions come from our deepest truth.
- When we are in the **Red Zone,** we are out of alignment with our deepest sense of self. In other words, we are not living our truth. The result is that we do not feel worthy.

- The Red and Rebirth Zones are merely perspectives until we decide we want to move from the Red to the Rebirth Zone and that there is a way to do so – at that point, the first step becomes the beginning of a journey to our greatest sense of self-worth and deepest truth.

Which part of the Red Zone or Rebirth Zone are you in? Study the diagram and notes below – do you recognise your Point A?

In the Red Zone, from Part 3: Journey of Seeking

Fear – An ego-inspired illusion of steep hills and rocky ground that may lead to a severe lack of action. It masquerades in many forms (see the nine base fears in *Part 2: Awareness*).

Translation to life: This is a feeling of overwhelm based on your perception that you are not able to take action and achieve your definition of success; that the task is too daunting and you might not have the ability to take it on.

Insecurity – a condition that slowly depletes a warrior's energy and perception of their own power, leading the warrior to believe that they have fallen into a black pit where no light will ever be present and no help is available.

Translation to life: The feeling that you're not good enough or that someone else is better suited to the task.

Failure – The false perception of a darkness so black that even thinking about its presence causes extreme exhaustion and discouragement. White noise often accompanies failure.

Translation to life: A misaligned perception that your past experiences have proven you don't have the ability to perform a certain task successfully. A feeling that you've tried, were not good enough and will never be good enough.

I mentioned in *Part 2: Awareness* that fear is a distrust of your own worth. Insecurity and a perception of failure also stem from that distrust of your worth, yet none of these three states of BE-ing is a bad thing. They are not negative – they serve as indicators by tuning you into your Point A and giving you direction towards your Point B.

In the Rebirth Zone

Imagination – The knowing that the world is open to you; it is the sparkle inside when you think about a dream you have or when a great idea occurs to you.

Vulnerability – The state of feeling comfortable about who you are, where you are and how you feel; BE-ing totally YOU in every interaction;

BE-ing free of opinions, expectations, circumstances, words, thoughts and actions that don't align with who you are.

Foundation – The state of BE-ing where you recognise your journey has had purpose and has built a solid foundation for you to BE your full potential; knowing that every step of your journey has held value, and that there is no such thing as failure.

RED ZONE	REBIRTH ZONE	FROM RED ZONE TO REBIRTH ZONE
Fear	Imagination	Learn to step into your **imagination** with excitement and readiness instead of being in a state of fear.
Insecurity	Vulnerability	BE in the space where you embrace your **vulnerability** and recognise its gifts, free of expectations, thoughts, words and actions that don't align with who you are.
Failure	Foundation	Use all your experiences as the **foundation** for BE-ing your potential, while recognising your strength, courage and growth in every experience you've had.

Chapter 29
THE UN-BECOMING PROCESS

The UN-Becoming process is the vehicle from your Point A to your Point B in the Rebirth Zone.

The Five Building Blocks of the UN-Becoming process

1. Education

True education is about crystallising all you've learned from every experience and recognising the value of this wisdom. The journey to self-worth is about embracing the foundation and path of your unique wisdom.

2. Meditation

Finding the stillness within allows you to access your creativity, your pioneering thoughts and the UN-explored possibility in your life. When you carve out time to spend with YOU, you're giving your entire BE-ing the message that you are worthy.

3. Gratitude

BE-ing in gratitude in any moment for anything gives you a feeling that you are taken care of; there is a sense of well-being and a feeling that you matter enough and are worthy enough to bask in this moment of well-being.

4. Connection

Connection and meditation go hand-in-hand. Connecting to Source (call it God within, Universe, Divine Presence, Higher Self, your centre, your heart or whatever resonates) allows you to access your inner guidance or intuition. This is a great self-care practice. It allows you to feel your alignment and worthiness.

5. Empathy

Empathy is defined as imagining yourself in someone else's shoes; feeling what they could be feeling, especially when they are in discomfort or pain. While there is value in doing this, for the UN-Becoming Process, I call on you to imagine yourself in someone else's shoes when they have the sense of feeling fulfilled, confident, abundant and free-spirited.

For example, you see a speaker on stage stepping into her full potential and touching the lives of thousands – how does she feel? If you haven't had that experience, you can create the feeling of BE-ing in your highest potential. You've had the feeling of doing something you love or having something you really want or feeling "in-the-zone". Create THAT feeling.

The best way to practise the building block of empathy is by going back to a moment in your life (it doesn't matter how far back or how recent that moment was) when you felt carefree, free-spirited, accomplished, confident or content. Recreate that feeling. Bring the sights, smells, sounds, tastes, and physical feelings back to you. It's not about the event you're remembering – it's about the feelings.

When you recreate your feeling of well-being, in that moment, your entire BE-ing believes in your abundance and happiness. You automatically step into the realm of UN-explored possibilities in your life.

How to apply the Five Building Blocks

1. When you feel "less than", recognise what base emotion in the Red Zone underlies what you are feeling. **If you don't know this immediately, make use of a Truth Journey to learn.**

The Truth Journey and how to use it:

Write about how you feel right now. What are your fears, your insecurities, your perceptions of yourself, your feelings of joy and excitement? **Your intention is to be in a space of moving forward and treating yourself with kindness and love. Each sentence should begin with: *The truth is that…***

Let the feelings flow and translate themselves into words. Don't think about what you're writing, and don't censor your feelings or the words that are flowing onto paper. A truth journey is a journey of the Soul, not a journey of the mind. The sentences might be scrambled, they might not align with who you are, but give them the respect of being what they are right now.

Examples:

- *The truth is that I believe there is much, much more in me to do and to give, and I don't know how to let it out of me.*
- *The truth is that I am in a good place right now, and for the first time I don't feel like a stranger in my skin.*
- *The truth is that I feel surrounded and engulfed by love in this moment, and I want it to last forever.*
- *The truth is that I am afraid of disappointing myself.*

You can also write a question that is troubling you to get clarity about your feelings, and use a Truth Journey to put your feelings into words – here is an example:

Why do I feel like there's a cloud hanging over my head?

The truth is that on some level I'm scared. I'm scared by my past. I'm scared that I don't have it in me to make something huge work; to create something big.

The truth is that I know I'm meant for something big. I know I'm Divinely Guided.

The truth is that I don't want to wait; I may be at my breaking point; I'm trying to hold it together. I can't.

The truth is that it's easier to imagine hardship and sadness than it is to imagine happiness.

The truth is that I'm at the beginning of an exciting new chapter in my life – and I'm creating my dream life.

Don't stop writing until you find yourself writing something in the spirit of moving forward and recognising your Light – that is the space of alignment.

Now find your Point A in the Red Zone using your Truth Journey. Are you in fear (read through the definition of fear above)? Are you feeling a sense of insecurity? Do you have a perception of failure about yourself? Do all three states play a part in how you are feeling?

2. Where in the Rebirth Zone do you want to move to? Study the diagram in Chapter 28: *Red Zone or Rebirth Zone*. Each of the three Red Zone points leads to a Rebirth Zone point. E.g. from fear, you would move to imagination; from insecurity you'd move to the point of vulnerability; and from the perception of failure, you'd move to foundation.

3. Apply any or all of the Five Building Blocks to the situation to move to your Point B:

    a. Education – Remind yourself that you are NOT defined by your experiences. The person who had that experience in the past is not the YOU who is present today. You have grown and evolved. You are now someone different. You cannot apply the experiences of someone else to *your* reality today. **List what you've learned and what education you've gained from your journey of evolution.** You've probably learned more than you give yourself credit for. As you discover this using the education building block, your confidence level climbs, and you're able to move from the perception of failure in the Red Zone to a feeling of having built the foundation for your inner fulfilment in the Rebirth Zone.

b. Meditation – Value your BE-ing in this moment. Allow your breathing to guide you into your space of inner peace. **Connect with that space where there is no white noise, no judgement and no thoughts that do not serve you.** This path to the Rebirth Zone is effective because you're freeing yourself from opinions, expectations, circumstances, words, thoughts and actions that don't align with who you are.

c. Gratitude – Find a reason to be in gratitude in this moment. If you don't feel a sense of gratitude within, what is the most basic reason you can be in appreciation for how you're feeling? Have you learned something that serves you well? Does the contrast help you see what you do and don't want? **Make a gratitude list of only those things you feel grateful for in the moment, even if it's only your heartbeat or breath. This is an exercise of feeling, not thinking.** The feeling of gratitude opens your heart to love and alignment, and your mind to possibility, guiding your path from the Red Zone to the Rebirth Zone.

d. Connection – **Connect to Source (call it whatever resonates with you – God within, Universe, Divine Presence, Higher Self, your centre, or your heart) through Divine Communication, prayer or thoughts of love.** The wisdom, peace and healing that comes from this connection helps you to recognise your self-worth. You realise that you are the Light. You feel the ONE-ness that connects all BE-ings. You are connecting with the deepest part of you that is UN-changing and will always be present; the energy part of you; the Source of your deepest truth. From this space, you're able to BE in the Rebirth Zone.

e. Empathy – Think about an experience you've had that empowered you or created a feeling of accomplishment, peace, or happiness. **Recreate THAT feeling. BE with that feeling and breathe it in.** It is the knowing that you are worthy to receive, that at your deepest level, the Rebirth Zone is where you are called to BE.

You don't have to use your own thoughts exclusively when you're applying the Five Building Blocks to your life. **You can also use resources such as books, videos, audios or live conversations to inspire your application of the Building Block(s) you've chosen to work with.**

For example, you can use a guided meditation audio when you've chosen the meditation or connection building blocks, and it may help to watch a two-minute heart-warming video before you use the gratitude building block. Use whatever resource enhances the Building Block you've chosen. Or you might not want to use any other resource at all. Tune in to your emotions, adapt to the physical space you're in, and work with your time constraints when choosing whether to use a resource that enhances your building block.

Real-life situations for applying the Five Building Blocks

Why would you use the five building blocks? How would you use them in your daily life?

In our human state, we always seem to need a reason for applying a life truth to our lives other than that we'll feel good when we apply it.

Feeling good doesn't seem to be enough – we've been so indoctrinated by the village that has collectively raised us to always have a bigger and nobler reason for doing something. Our Point B, we are taught, must have a higher purpose, and how we feel should fade into the background.

I feel called to add various situations where it would help to apply the five building blocks so that you can use them to move to a higher vibration. At a higher vibration, you feel good and more capable of fulfilling what you know as your calling. Feeling good, however is our priority right now.

At this time in our world living out our potential as individuals will give birth to an era of co-creation, collaboration, peace and unity. In sharing this wisdom, I am fulfilling my own potential and calling. I've felt as if something is missing from this beautiful book that has come to me in a way I could never have predicted. What's missing is the part of me that I've been hiding; the part of me that was, for so long, seeking acceptance and was afraid of being shunned, ridiculed or messing up the depth of the message I was called to give.

I am not afraid anymore. I have no wall of resistance (probably because my body feels physically weak as I include this Guidance – my body is detoxifying and I don't have the energy to analyse or to counter the voice of Source speaking to me now).

<u>How I have applied the Five Building Blocks in my life:</u>

- I am an Akashic Records reader, doing readings for individuals, organisations and businesses. Through these readings, I tap into the realms of what we call past, present and future. Clients ask about any aspect of life, including relationships, health, career, finances, spirituality, and messages from loved ones on the Other Side. They experience an inner peace through this Divine Guidance that empowers them with their present choices and understanding of their lives. **I use one or more of the Five Building Blocks to BE at a higher vibration before doing a reading.**

- When clients request an UN-Becoming session to access their life's purpose more fully, **I walk them through the applicable Building Blocks.**

- A while ago, I was having a conversation with a fellow entrepreneur. She filled me in about parts of her life experience that influenced her work. "I've been in corporate for fifteen years," she said. I observed myself shrinking back, thinking about how my work experience felt less rich. It took a few seconds to come back to centre, realising that my experience wasn't less rich – it was just different. I silently asked myself for a description about how my life experience had influenced my work. It flowed from me organically: I grew up in medicine. I was a caregiver in my home for about twelve years and worked in the natural healing realm for twenty-six years. I've also been an educator in different capacities for that long. I used the education Building Block to list my life education that has been the foundation for my work today. **When I don't feel the value of my life experiences, this is the Building Block I use to remind me of how every experience was a brick in building the solid foundation of my dreams and life purpose.**

- **I use the gratitude Building Block many mornings before I get out of bed.** It is the simplest way to raise my vibration in the moment and set the tone for a fulfilling and peaceful day.

Different ways in which individuals use the Five Building Blocks of UN-Becoming:

- Writers use the Building Blocks to raise their vibrations to where they can channel the messages and words they feel called to give their readers.
- Speakers use the Building Blocks to translate Divine Guidance into words, speaking their truth to their audience, simply and authentically.
- Parents and educators use the Building Blocks to create a good-feeling energy space in which their children can thrive. UN-stressed parents and educators are able to create an environment of happy and relaxed children who start learning to integrate the Building Blocks too.
- Individuals use the Building Blocks to build deeper relationships with their partners, leading to constructive and connection-oriented communication, a higher collective vibration, and a stronger relationship.
- In the work environment, individuals use the Building Blocks to bring their best selves to the table by coming from a high vibration.
- Teams and organisations use the Building Blocks to build a cohesive community with a culture of peace, unity and growth.

- Individuals and organisations use the Building Blocks to resolve difficult situations that may lead to conflict.

- The Building Blocks are used to raise the collective vibration in conversations to inspire peace, unity and co-creation as a community

- Many people feel called to commune with our non-human global family. They use the Building Blocks to move to a higher vibration so that they are able to receive messages and communicate with creatures as well as nature elders such as rocks, trees, plants, our air, water, soil, and our own Mother Earth.

- When individuals feel called to a higher purpose or a big dream, they use the Building Blocks to raise their vibrations to the place where they feel worthy of their dreams and capable of taking the next step forward.

Chapter 30
BREAKING THROUGH THE BELIEF SYSTEM OF FEELING UNWORTHY

Often, it is not the path to living our truths that feels missing for us – it is the fact that we haven't given ourselves permission to live in our greatest sense of self-worth. We have the UN-Becoming Process and the Five Building Blocks of UN-Becoming, but we don't leave Point A because we don't feel worthy enough to take that first step. We feel we don't deserve the opportunity. We need to break through our flawed belief system to begin the journey.

The premise

Deserve: To prove worthy of receiving because of actions taken or criteria fulfilled.

From this thinking, you must earn the right to journey to Point B. If you don't feel worthy of the right to journey, you can't get to where you show up for yourself at your highest vibration because you don't feel deserving of getting to this point. Therefore, you can't show up for the world at your highest level of BE-ing either, and you can't increase the vibration in the world as you may feel called to do.

Why the concept of deserving and earning is not aligned with your deepest truth

The idea that you must earn your worthiness is ego-based thinking. It means that some people are worthy and some aren't; that some are supposed to get and some aren't. Who decides that? Why would it be so? Who told us that this was the rule? If this is our thinking, when did it start and why?

What if we are working with the wrong set of rules? It's like knowing you must create a hole in the ground, but you don't see a spade or know that such an implement is available. All you can see is a spoon, and you believe the spoon's purpose is to dig.

How do we change our limiting beliefs about ourselves, our abilities and the rules we believe we have to live by? We start by questioning the foundation of our beliefs (the rules we thought applied to us); we start with the very first brick – when that crumbles, the bastions of our self-imposed limitations follow suit.

Let's bring this esoteric idea home with real-life applications about the concepts of earning, deserving, and worthiness. From *Part 1: Truth Within,* "**When shame, anger or guilt accompanies a thought about yourself or your experience, that thought cannot be heart-centred and is therefore not aligned with your truth.**" If you think of yourself as not deserving worthiness, how do you feel? Do you feel a sense of shame about who you are? Do you feel angry because you feel left out of the gift of receiving? Do you feel guilty because you believe you should earn more worthiness through better behaviour?

Whatever your feelings, you don't feel good about yourself with this type of thinking. It is clearly not aligned with your deepest truth, and it is not heart-centred. What if you think about a friend who is going through a tough time in terms of the concept of deserving? Do you think they need to earn the right to have a better time in life? Do you think they are simply not among the few chosen worthy individuals in the world? And what makes it so? What would they need to do to earn the right to have good things happen to them?

There is no logic with the earning and deserving mentality. How about putting the spoon aside and considering that there may be a spade?

How about being open to the knowing that every BE-ing is worthy?

How about dispensing with the idea that external circumstances, opinions or expectations determine your worthiness?

When you align with the truth that you are worthy because every BE-ing is inherently worthy, how does that feel? You are an expression of the Universe, and what a bountiful, worthy Universe we are part of! Consider that – you are the contributor and the contribution to the Universe's majesty. When you feel that, it's like taking two wires of a broken electrical circuit and allowing the wires to touch each other and complete the circuit – there is heat, there is light, there is connection and alignment.

How do we complete the circuit in real life? How do we feel and live by the knowing that we are worthy? How do we do that in our daily lives when our repeated pattern may be a belief of feeling undeserving and unworthy?

Real-life Solutions

OBSERVATION:
1. Notice your fear, insecurity or perception of your own impending failure, and observe the context. What topic were you thinking about that caused the fear to surface?
2. Identify the belief you have about yourself in relation to the belief you hold about the situation. Do you feel the situation is difficult to navigate, or do you feel you lack the capability to navigate it?
3. Are you having a physical reaction – is it tight in your throat or chest, or is there an uncomfortable sinking feeling in your abdomen? Are you sweating or breathing faster? Are you finding it difficult to breathe deeply?

PHYSICAL SOLUTION:
1. Bring calmness and Peace into your awareness by consciously slowing your breathing down.
2. Remember a feeling that makes you smile – a baby in your life hugging you or holding your hand, a pet cuddling up against you, the good belly-laugh you had. Feel that feeling again and again.
3. Use the Building Block of meditation or connection – you may feel called to listen to music that feels calming and breathe

with it. You may feel called to listen to a guided meditation, or you may decide to go into your own version of meditation.

THOUGHT SOLUTION DAILY:

1. Treat yourself as worthy; you are Source energy. Every BE-ing is Source energy and is worthy of being treated as such. Remind yourself that you are birthed and nurtured by a worthy mother – Mother Earth. You are an expression of our majestic Universe. The conditions of Mother Earth and our Universe support your physical life – you're THAT worthy.

2. BE who you feel you are called to be – act as if you feel completely UN-limited and worthy of BE-ing who you want to see in the mirror or the YOU in your most joyful visualisations about your future self.

3. Remind yourself that any thought or feeling that is out of alignment with Source within, is out of alignment with your deepest truth. Your deepest truth comes from Source within.

4. Have compassion for the human BE-ing that is YOU. Be kind to yourself.

5. Bombard your mind with material that confirms your worthiness – use any or all of the Five Building Blocks. Use your thoughts, books, videos, audios or live conversations to inspire your application of the Building Block(s) you've chosen to work with.

Chapter 31
SIX KEYS TO MANIFESTING TRUTH

What is truth? Expanding on the definition in *Part 1: Truth Within*, truth is synonymous with alignment, self-worth, living in the Rebirth Zone; recognising yourself as a BE-ing of Light.

Light a match in what you perceive as darkness. Can you now describe your surroundings as being in light or being in darkness? Focus on the match or focus on the darkness – what you focus on is what you will see, even though the Light is ever-present.

What is manifesting? It is the alignment of your thoughts, words, actions, interactions, and emotions with your deepest truth and your greatest sense of self-worth.

Staying in the space of manifesting your truth is a mindset; a knowing that wherever you are in a specific moment (the Red or the Rebirth Zone), you can step into aligning with your deepest truth. The Six Keys below will help you align with and physically manifest your deepest truth.

1. Home is within

Circumstances and physical spaces that are ideal are not an essential condition for manifesting truth. You create your reality from the inside out. Your thoughts and the emotions attached to those thoughts (the energy space you come from) determine whether you manifest your truth. Create a sense of "home" within you – the feelings of love, contentment and gratitude.

2. There are no missteps

If you were driving to a city three hours away and the route to your destination, although safe enough, was a dirt road with potholes, would you still go on the journey? Or would you turn back and make peace with not going where you wanted to go. You'd probably go because your goal is to be at your destination. What if, a few months later, you looked back on your journey and discovered that there was indeed a smoother road you could have taken – would you consider your journey a mistake? It got you where you needed to go, regardless of your road not being smooth, so how could it be a misstep? The journey, and your discovery of the smoother route, has been an experience of learning and growth. It served your purpose. Walk your path, knowing that there are no missteps.

3. The joy is in the journey

We can go back to childhood to see the impact of this.

Think of something you learned to do and loved to do as a child, e.g. riding a bike, learning to swim, learning to read or learning to do equations. When you enjoy an activity, you probably enjoyed the journey of learning the skill, as well as your progress along the way. What was the attached emotion when you were learning it? What was the feeling when you mastered the skill? Keep the emotion of that memory so that it can serve you when using the UN-Becoming Building Block of empathy. You DO know the emotions of feeling successful, accomplished, and happy! Go back to the joy of the journey to BE in the space of manifesting your truth into physical reality. When you know you CAN, you have journeyed to the Rebirth Zone.

4. YOU are the experience

If you see a situation as the experience, you are more emotionally charged. There are always two poles – you are either in the Red Zone or in the Rebirth Zone. When you feel good about a situation, the emotions work in your favour. When you perceive the situation as negative, the attached emotion keeps you stuck in the Red Zone, until you decide to change your thoughts.

Consider that the situation doesn't hold importance – it is about how you see yourself in that moment. Meditate to see yourself in love, with love and of love. (See suggested meditation below.) When you are in this space, it is easier to journey from the Red Zone to the Rebirth Zone because it is not the situation that has to change – it is simply you aligning with who you are in your deepest sense of self. A perceived negative situation experienced with emotion has an inertia attached to it. Seeing the truth of who you are is the force that moves you to the Rebirth Zone. *The Truth-Walker's Journey* is about how you walk the path from recognising this to knowing who you are constantly, even in your most misaligned moments in the Red Zone. You are the experience – the situation is only a manifestation of your perceptions, whether your perceptions are aligned with your truth or distorted by your ego.

5. BE

Stop trying so hard – BE-ing aligned with our truth came naturally and easily in childhood. As we grew up, we allowed ourselves to view our lives through the filters of the village that raised us. We took on their fears and insecurities, and this is how we stopped seeing the Light that was our core.

As an adult, the moral dilemmas we experience are the contrast between what comes naturally, and the expectations that are not in alignment with our deepest truth. To BE means to find your Guidance within and act on it despite the sea of white noise around you.

6. Your journey is your own

Your journey is from your personal Point A of the moment to your Point B (where your thoughts, words, actions and interactions have shifted into alignment with your deepest sense of self). Even though there are many different paths and many sets of footprints on these paths, trust your own choice of Point B and the path you've selected to get you there.

Meditation to BE in the Six Keys mindset

Breathe and meditate on this message when you need a reminder of who you are at your core:

I am Divine Truth.

I am Love.

I am Light.

I am Peace.

*I am Divine Inspiration manifested into all that **is** right now.*

I am the experience.

I flow.

I am above and beyond circumstances, filters, perspectives, and emotions.

I am Divine Wisdom and Infinite Possibility.

I am every hope, dream and Inspired thought rolled into the power of now.

I AM.

Summary – How to manifest truth in your life

1. Use your emotions as an indicator of your Point A.
2. Use the Five Building Blocks of UN-Becoming to be aligned with your deepest truth.
3. Allow your thoughts, words, and actions to align with your truth.
4. BE in the Six Keys mindset.

Chapter 32
CREATING A NEW DEFAULT IN 30 DAYS

Do you wish you had a wand to get you from Point A to Point B? You do. You can immerse yourself in your journey to UN-Become who you are not and live in your greatest sense of self-worth and deepest truth. If you choose to do this, here are the steps:

Laying the foundation

Think about the questions below:

- What is your deepest intention?
- What is your greatest purpose?
- What are you inspired to let go of?
- What story are you telling yourself that you are inspired to UN-tell?

Read your journal entries for the *Action Sessions* in *Part 2: Awareness*. Your wisdom will help you answer the questions above.

Premise for creating a new default in 30 days

- There is no past or future – I am in the NOW. I have the power to recreate my past and create my future. I have the power to UN-create anything that does not serve me.
- I will show up for ME so that I can show up for the world at my best.

The path to showing up for YOU

- Apply the Five Building Blocks of UN-Becoming to your life.
- Break through the belief system of feeling unworthy.
- Use the Six Keys to stay in the mindset of manifesting truth.

The practice of how to create a new default in 30 days

Five times a day, for five to ten minutes, focus on one of the Five Building Blocks of UN-Becoming (Education, Meditation, Gratitude, Connection or Empathy), applying it to your life or to a situation in your now. The times listed below are a suggestion – you can apply this practice in any way it fits into your life.

- Time 1: **6 – 9am**
- Time 2: **10am – 12pm**
- Time 3: **1 – 3pm**
- Time 4: **4 – 7pm**
- Time 5: **8 – 10pm**

In each of the above time slots, every day:

1. Put aside **five or ten minutes of dedicated time.**
2. Choose **one of the Five Building Blocks** of UN-Becoming.
3. Use a stimulus (see examples below) to help you focus on the Building Block and BE in the mindset of the Six Keys to manifest truth.
4. Explore your chosen Building Block in a thought exercise or written exercise, or even in the form of drawing, collaging or video journaling.

Examples

If you have chosen the Building Block of gratitude, do one or more of the following:

Explore your own empowering thoughts if you are already in the Six Keys mindset of manifesting truth. Create a Soul Collage focusing on gratitude, or write in your journal, listing your feelings of gratitude.

- Watch a video (a quick personal development video) that inspires you to feel gratitude.
- Listen to an audio recording that gets you into the space of appreciation.
- Read material that helps you to feel gratitude – e.g. read an inspiring story about human courage that touches your heart.

Repeat the process in each of your five time slots for 30 days. You can choose the same Building Block or a different one for each time slot – go with what feels right for you.

How to find your Point A in any given moment

- **Your thoughts** – distinguish between self-empowering thoughts and self-defeating thoughts. Consciously think thoughts that support you.

- **Your emotions** – use them as indicators of whether your thoughts are self-empowering and connected to who you are at your deepest level.

What to do when you find your past baggage clouding your now

Do a bypass – sometimes a surgeon does a bypass for a cardiac patient in an emergency. It's not ideal but in the now, it's a solution that allows the patient to live with a functioning circulatory system. The proper solution is for the patient to change their lifestyle and contribute to their well-being through taking Inspired action. The bypass is a stopgap that buys more time while the patient implements the actual solution.

Similarly, sometimes it is least damaging to bypass the baggage and accompanying feelings of the past, to BE in the now without baggage or disempowering thoughts. We don't need to relive the past or use it to define who we are. The proper solution is to recognise the baggage and disempowering feelings or thoughts when they surface, becoming aware of the situations in which they make themselves known. With this wisdom, we can create a new default in thirty days using the Building Blocks of UN-Becoming.

Chapter 33
HONOURING YOUR BE-ING

I have walked the labyrinth many times in this lifetime, sometimes unknowingly, sometimes in awareness. I have done so physically with conscious intention, but mostly mentally and spiritually. I enter the labyrinth to slay the minotaur – my greatest fears, insecurities and perceptions of failure. As I reach the centre of the labyrinth, where I am in the greatest awareness about my deepest intention, I reach the point of enlightenment. I meet the minotaur, face-to-face. For the first time, I, in my evolved state, see the light in the monster's eyes. It ceases to be a monster – that perception melts away and there is only light. I am not here to slay a monster but to recognise and connect with my centre, my Soul, my BE-ing. I AM the Light. It was my fear that created the image of the monster. The darkness has only been there because I have not seen my light before. I have not honoured the Light within me.

What is the act of honouring your BE-ing?

Your BE-ing supports your intention, and your mind, body and spirit each support your BE-ing. In the act of UN-Becoming who you are not, know that it is your mind, body and spirit that co-create to live out your deepest truth and your greatest sense of self-worth. Each of these precious parts of you enables you to heal to your next evolutionary level. Honouring each part of you for its collaboration in your journey is an act of honouring and connecting with your deepest truth.

Letters to mind, body and spirit as an act of honouring your BE-ing

There are many ways to honour your mind, body and spirit, but writing a letter of gratitude to each is powerful. In the act of writing and feeling the appreciation as you write, you reactivate the knowing that you are not simply your mind or your body – you are a BE-ing of Light in this lifetime supported by every component of YOU. The thought is empowering. It is the knowing that you, the human BE-ing, do not walk unsupported or alone.

Write the letters to mind, body and spirit in a journal or on writing paper, and keep the letters. When you need a reminder of who you are and the support you have available to you, read them and meditate on them. Reading the letters with meaning is a way of honouring your BE-ing, A time will come when you've grown beyond the words in your letters, and they don't express who you are, fully. Carve out time to honour your BE-ing again and write new letters.

There is no right or wrong way to express yourself – let the words flow from you. If letter writing doesn't resonate with you, create a video, audio recording, Soul Collage, drawing, painting or any other creative way of honouring your mind, body and spirit. I am sharing my letters with you below:

Honouring your mind

Dear Amazing mind,

I thank you for giving me the power of thought and for breathing life into each thought. Thank you for giving me a glimpse into me BE-ing my potential. Thank you also for protecting me from the reality I don't want to create by giving me insight into what that would look like.

Your logic and sound reasoning have carried me through fears, insecurities and negative perceptions of myself. You always assure me that you have the tools to help get me to the next level and there is no darkness that I can't step out of by starting with a few empowering thoughts. Even in the contrasting thoughts of darkness, you show me the seeds of my purpose and desires – I appreciate that.

As I spark my creativity through this letter to you, I am aware that you are collaborating with me to make this letter happen; to breathe my spirit into these words on the page. I honour you for that, dear Mind… and I am in appreciation.

Honouring your body

Dearest Basic Units of Life – the cells that make up my beautiful and miraculous body,

Firstly, thank you! Thank you for uniting to create the physical vessel that houses my BE-ing. Thank you for rising to the challenge of nourishing me, despite the fact that you don't always receive optimum raw materials for this purpose.

I appreciate the miracles you have created and continue to create in my body – my beating heart, my lungs filling with air, my temperature, homeostasis. Thank you for creating a home for me – one that houses my tears, my laughter, my highs and my lows.

I realise there are times I mistreat you consciously and unconsciously. Sometimes it is because I am self-absorbed and tangled in my own ego, and at other times I don't realise the damage I inflict, or even that I am inflicting anything negative on you at all. That sounds horrible.

My commitment to you from here on is that I will make a conscious effort to consider you in my thoughts, words and actions. I will use my emotions as indicators so that I know what care you need and how to nourish you with my thoughts and physical actions. I will care for you more than I care about being right or getting into that whirlpool of ego. Bringing myself down brings you down, and it's not okay to treat you this way.. I will raise myself up at every opportunity since I know that is what you need. I may fall short of my promises from time to time, but I commit to you that I will do the best I know how to do in every moment, I will learn from every error, and I will grow and evolve.

You haven't asked anything of me and you have given so much. I am in gratitude for the gift of my body, the physical home of my BE-ing. I love you. May you grow and flourish, and I will do all in my power to help you in that.

Honouring your spirit

Dearest Centre of my BE-ing,

You are the eternal part of me – the ME that has been through the journeys of past, present and future that my present self doesn't even remember. You have been my teacher, my Guide, my Connection to all that is, lifetime after lifetime. My words right now seem so paltry because our communication has always been beyond words and beyond the constraints of the Earthly Realm. You are the part of me that is Love and ultimate enlightenment. You Guide me through your ever-present Light and your quest for the Peace of my entire BE-ing.

I breathe my gratitude to you now. Feel me honouring you, finding your presence within and BE-ing with your Love and Light. Your Connection is everything to me.

I AM... always because of you. I honour the journey.

Namaste.

Part 5: BE-ING

Your UN-Becoming has UN-earthed a way of BE-ing that aligns with who you are at your core. The next step is to integrate this way of BE-ing into your world. The Truth-Walker's Manifesto is a guide to doing that. It is the reminder to find and align with your deepest truth despite life's white noise, and to contribute to a world where every BE-ing has the freedom to do the same.

- Principles 1 – 6 are based on one or more of the Six Keys to Manifesting Truth (See *Part 4: UN-Becoming*).

- Every principle includes an expansion, a meditation, the essence of the meditation, an Inspired action, and the meaning of the meditation for your life.

- A suggestion is to read through the Manifesto every day and meditate on one principle. This will be an eight-day journey. Thereafter, take a further eight days and meditate on whichever principle resonates with you each day. It may lead you to re-explore *Part 4: UN Becoming*. There are no rules. Go with your gut!

Chapter 34
THE TRUTH-WALKER'S MANIFESTO

1. I AM mind-body-spirit, birthed from, of, on, Mother Earth. I AM the personification of 13.8 billion years of evolution. (The Awakening)

2. I choose to journey inward, listen deeply, and connect with Source within.* (The Journey)

3. I choose to BE my deepest truth, bringing the energy of love and respect to every BE-ing, in every interaction, including interactions with myself. (The BE-ing)

4. I choose to free my BE-ing from the constraints of expectations, approval, definitions, circumstances, thoughts, words, actions and reactions that don't feel aligned with my deepest truth. (The Freeing)

5. I choose to consciously heal to my next evolutionary level of BE-ing. (The "Healing to")

---

* Call it whatever resonates with you: Divine Guidance, Higher Self, my centre, my heart, God within.

6. I AM interconnected with every BE-ing on Mother Earth. I choose to contribute to our collective evolution through my own conscious evolution. (The Embracing)

7. I respect that every BE-ing has the right to live out their Divine truth in, with and from freedom. (The Recognising)

8. I choose to BE part of creating a world where every BE-ing can live out their Divine truth in, with and from freedom. (The Contributing)

Chapter 35
PRINCIPLE 1: THE AWAKENING

I AM mind-body-spirit, birthed from, of, on, Mother Earth. I AM the personification of 13.8 billion years of evolution.

Expansion

This principle recognises and honours the entirety of your BE-ing. It creates the space for you to find and connect with your deepest truth.

The basis of the principle from the Six Keys to Manifesting Truth

Home is within.

Meditation

*The truth that is you, is perfect. Perfectly you. It asks nothing of you. It is the answer to your every question. It is the answer to your most important question: who am I? Who am **I**?*

And when you ask this question, what is the answer you receive from your heart? What speaks to you in a way that feels like home?

BE with that. Take in the silence. Honour the silence. Honour your BE-ing – your body, your mind, your spirit. You are the personification of 13.8 billion years of evolution. When you have an inner knowing of this, your answer will rise from within, loud and clear.

Breathe, love, act, serve. Allow your body, mind and spirit to meet and fuse in the sound of your own, deliberate breath…

Body – the physical manifestation of the breath…

Mind – the deliberate, purposeful decision to inhale and exhale…

Spirit – the house of the Divine within; the true power of BE-ing, the Source of that which we call life and from where the breath of life comes…

Do you know your own truth? Can you trace the pattern on your age-old Soul? BE with that.

The essence

This meditation is the recognition of your BE-ing in mind, body, and spirit form. It is the honouring of your deepest truth from the mind, body and spirit perspectives; the recognition that the entirety of your BE-ing supports your deepest truth.

Inspired action

After BE-ing with this meditation, set an intention for your day that is aligned with your truth. Do this by asking:

- How may my BE-ing, in its entirety, support my mind?
- How may my BE-ing, in its entirety, support my body?
- How may my BE-ing, in its entirety, support my spirit?
- What may I know about my BE-ing?

Write whatever comes to you.

The meaning for your life

When you acknowledge the connection of body, mind and spirit, and the entirety of your BE-ing, you're creating the space to connect your thoughts, emotions, words and actions to your deepest truth.

Chapter 36
PRINCIPLE 2: THE JOURNEY

I choose to journey inward, listen deeply,
and connect with Source within.

Expansion

Through Principle 2, you're setting the intention to find your deepest truth in the moment and breathe it in. You're giving permission to YOU to explore the journey within and know that this journey holds value and purpose.

The basis of the principle from the Six Keys to Manifesting Truth

- Home is within.
- The joy is in the journey.

Meditation

Breathe in, feel the breath entering your body, then release it slowly. Repeat this process.

Collaborate with your breath.

This moment is yours. This action is of your choosing.

Let all that is around you fade away. Allow your thoughts to wander in and out, of their own accord. Let go. Trust the process of letting go. Allow your breathing to come naturally.

What truth is in your heart? Allow it to come to the surface when it is ready.

Take the next five minutes and just **BE**. **BE *you***. *BE at peace, whatever peace means to you.*

The essence

As you let go and trust the process, you're creating space for your truth to come into your awareness. **It is in the silence of peace that the truth of the heart finds a voice.**

Inspired action

- After your five minutes of silence, go on a Truth Journey (as described in *Part 4: The UN-Becoming*). Before you do this, ask with intention: *What is the truth deep within me that I AM aligned with in this moment?*

The meaning for your life

Five minutes of silence can change your life. If you haven't taken time for yourself in a while, you may feel as if you're giving yourself a much needed emotional hug. In aligning with your deepest truth, you are caring for *you*. This gesture raises your vibration and you're able to bring a higher level of energy to your BE-ing and to your interactions with your fellow BE-ings.

Chapter 37
PRINCIPLE 3: THE BE-ING

I choose to BE my deepest truth, bringing the energy of love and respect to every BE-ing, in every interaction, including interactions with myself.

Expansion

Principle 3 highlights the Inspired action one takes to connect with one's deepest truth in the moment and to bring this truth to one's conscious awareness.

The basis of the principle from the Six Keys to Manifesting Truth

- YOU are the experience.
- BE.

Meditation

Lie on your back (savasana pose in yoga). Ensure your back is flat and your shoulders are touching the floor if possible.

Relax your body.

Feel your breath slowing down.

Put your right hand over your heart and feel the rhythmic pulsing of this remarkable organ.

Feel the sensation of the beat on your hand.

What does your heart want right here, right now?

What is the truth that is in your heart and longs to be heard?

The essence

- It is empowering to give voice to one's truth. This action is a form of respecting oneself deeply.
- When you give voice to your truth, you are communicating with yourself. Respect this interaction by giving it a sense of stillness and taking the time you need.
- Truth comes from the deepest part of one's BE-ing – Source within, Divine Guidance, your centre, your heart, your Higher Self, God within. The words that come from your truth feel loving, and reflect who you are at the deepest level.

Inspired action

Write today's truth in a journal (or type or record it on your phone). Re-visit these words a few times during the day. BE with the meaning of the words. This is a way of keeping your truth in your awareness so that your thoughts, words and actions throughout the day reflect your truth.

The meaning for your life

Thinking, speaking and acting in alignment with your truth means you're coming from a place of love and respect – from this space you are more creative, productive and solution-oriented. You're able to have clarity about what resonates with you and what doesn't. Decisions are easier to make because they either feel right or they don't, and you're able to recognise the difference.

Chapter 38
PRINCIPLE 4: THE FREEING

I choose to free my BE-ing from the constraints of expectations, approval, definitions, circumstances thoughts, words, actions and reactions that don't feel aligned with my deepest truth.

Expansion

Through Principle 4 you are keeping your deepest truth as the foundation of every interaction you have, knowing that you are freeing yourself for the journey to your highest potential.

The basis of the principle from the Six Keys to Manifesting Truth

- Home is within.
- YOU are the experience.

- Your journey is your own.
- BE

Meditation

Sit down in a relaxed position.

Take the index and third fingers of your right hand to your left wrist, and feel your pulse.

Take three deep breaths as you do this. Then breathe naturally to your own rhythm.

Feel the rhythm of your pulse and your breath.

You are in touch with the essence of your physical body.

Go deeper. In this space of your pulsing rhythm, feel the essence of who you are...

Stay in this space for five minutes. Ask your Inner Voice for any message that you need right now. Honour the message and honour your Inner Voice as message-giver.

The essence

- The interaction you have most often is the one with self. You can choose to let go of thoughts, words and actions that do not serve you or align with your deepest truth. Honour your BE-ing by connecting with your truth, through Source within.

- Voicing your truth to your fellow BE-ings is not about confessing everything that is in your heart. Share what you feel called to share at the time you feel called to share it, and with the person with whom it feels right to share (see *Part 1: Truth Within* – reread *The Energy of Truth*). Free yourself from the need to validate who you are.

Inspired action

- Write a letter to yourself today, connecting with your deepest truth. Before doing so, set the intention that you want to connect with Source within, and allow the messages you need to surface on a conscious, physical level. Know that BE-ing who you are is the highest service you can give to yourself and your world.

- If you feel called, write such a letter to yourself every day for the next seven days, feeling the alignment of your conscious communication with the voice of your deepest truth.

The meaning for your life

Voicing your truth is liberating. It feels empowering. When you communicate from your deepest truth as a default, you will no longer seek validation for your thoughts and feelings.

Chapter 39
PRINCIPLE 5: THE "HEALING TO"

I choose to consciously heal to my next evolutionary level of BE-ing.

Expansion

This principle acknowledges healing as a natural process of life. You are not healing FROM something that you don't want. You are healing TO your next evolutionary level. As evolving BE-ings, we are always healing.

The basis of the principle from the Six Keys to Manifesting Truth

- There are no missteps
- The joy is in the journey.
- BE.

Meditation

Breathe in and BE in your own heart space. It is the space of silence, Divinity, creation and the essence of you.

In this moment, feel and know who you are. You will know who you are because it feels like home to you.

What is the deepest feeling you have? Acknowledge it; respect it.

BE with your deepest essence for the next sixty seconds.

Now pick up a pencil and write all that is inside you. Alternatively, draw or paint it, or express it in any way that resonates with the truth of who you are – dance it, sing it, breathe it; BE it in any way you like.

Acknowledge the "Healing to" process about to take place within – it is the connection between the womb of BE-ing and the birthing of evolution.

The essence

I knocked on the door of my Soul. "Enter," my Soul whispered. I walked in, reverently in my bare feet and closed the door, for it was a place whose sanctity was to be respected; whose space was to be graced only by the essence of me; whose continuous process of evolving was to be trusted, for the process would support my every dream.

- When you align with Source within, there is only truth. The kaleidoscope of movement that occurs in your dance with your world is no longer there. You feel home in the essence of YOU, and you trust in your healing to your next evolutionary level.

- In this space, there is no 'if' or 'because' or any other limit or condition. There is only the truth of you. It is all you, and it is beautiful.
- Alignment takes place when you connect with yourself in the space of silence, away from the duality of your world. Your thoughts and feelings determine whether and how intimately you can connect.

Inspired action

Ask yourself daily:

- What do I feel?
- Is this who I AM and is this feeling mine?
- What am I healing to?

The meaning for your life

When you are BE-ing YOU, there is a feeling of well-being that washes over you – you feel a sense of gratitude for who you are. You feel empowered, strong, capable, creative, productive and in the zone. It is from this space that you consciously see yourself healing to your next evolutionary level and know its value.

Chapter 40
PRINCIPLE 6: THE EMBRACING

I AM interconnected with every BE-ing on Mother Earth. I choose to contribute to our collective evolution through my own conscious evolution.

Expansion

Principle 6 is the awareness of your interconnectedness with your world in every situation – your thoughts, words, actions and interactions are a contribution to the evolution of our collective.

The basis of the principle from the Six Keys to Manifesting Truth

- Home is within
- YOU are the experience.
- BE

Meditation

Sit comfortably on the ground, or close to the ground. Press your palms together at your heart centre.

Feel the silence around you and the Peace within.

Visualise yourself floating up to the ceiling or sky and looking down at your seated body right now. Observe yourself compassionately and lovingly.

The part of you looking down on your seated body is beyond any circumstance or situation. That part of you has the power to shift your entire BE-ing, and with it, your reality. As you shift your personal reality, you shift the reality of your world. Mother Earth lovingly shifts with you…through you…

BE with the feeling of who you are – Infinite Potential, Peace, Love, Creator of Possibility. You are all of it and more. You are an expression of our ever-evolving Universe.

When you are ready, float back to your seated body with the knowing of who you are.

The essence

You are the observer of change, the participant in change, and the creator of change. You are transformed through your calling and Inspired action to create change. Through your transformation, the world is different. The power of creating a better world is yours. You have been birthed of, from and on Mother Earth, and you are now consciously leading her "Healing to" process to her next evolutionary level.

Inspired action

- Briefly make a note of any situation that is worrying you.

- You have two choices – you can dissolve into the circumstances and allow them to determine your feelings, or you can take yourself out of the equation and recognise yourself as the observer of change, as well as participant in and creator of change.

- In this moment, are your feelings and responses determined by circumstances?

- How can you be YOU regardless of external circumstances?

- How can you BE the creator of change and evolution amidst the circumstances? How can you UN-create the circumstances through changing your perspective?

The meaning for your life

When you realise you have the power to change and to create change, external circumstances are not a factor in your growth. The circumstances are simply the medium in which you are BE-ing YOU. You can BE YOU in any set of circumstances. Your journey is beyond the here and now that you see. You are Infinite Possibility. You ARE the change.

Chapter 41
PRINCIPLE 7: THE RECOGNISING

I respect that every BE-ing has the right to live out their Divine truth in, with and from freedom.

Expansion

Principle 7 honours the right of every BE-ing to live from their deepest truth.

Meditation

Sit or lie down comfortably and breathe deeply.

Visualise three seedlings planted alongside one another. They are luscious and green with potential. Each has the mark of hope.

See each seedling growing, each becoming stronger and its cells becoming more in number and more specialised. Each seedling is becoming a plant. Each is growing in a unique way and at a different pace. Appreciate the structure and growth of each plant – see the miracle in each as it manifests its potential into the now.

Which plant has more value? Which is more entitled to grow? Which has the right to the best nutrients from the soil? Each of the seedlings is a miracle of life – a gift to the planet. Each has the right to the nourishment that it needs. Each enriches the earth with its gift of giving and receiving gases, and its contribution to the ecosystem.

Access appreciation and gratitude for each seedling and send out an intention for the well-being of each. Know that each seedling contributes to your well-being as you contribute to its well-being.

BE with this feeling for a minute, and as you breathe, feel the gift that each seedling has contributed to your life in this moment...

The essence

Just as each plant has the right to manifest its potential and live the truth of its existence, we human BE-ings have this right too. There is value in every BE-ing living out their truth.

Just as each plant's growth contributes to the ecosystem in which it exists, as well as to Mother Earth's evolution, our growth as individual human BE-ing adds value to our collective growth as a global community. Each of us, through of our existence, produces a ripple effect we are often not aware of. We are the nourishers, the nourished, and the nourishment of our world.

Inspired action

Ask yourself these questions with intention:

- What do I want to contribute to my world right now?
- What do I want to receive from my world right now?
- What Inspired action can I take today to give and receive this nourishment?

Make a note of your answers.

The meaning for your life

When we respect the right of every BE-ing to live out their deepest truth, we acknowledge that every BE-ing nourishes our world and contributes to its collective growth. It is an acknowledgement that we value these contributions and honour them, even when we don't understand them because they're different to our own contributions.

We don't exist in a vacuum, and our potential cannot be transformed into physical form in a vacuum. We are each contributor and contribution. Even contrasting views contribute to our evolution. It is the right of each BE-ing to manifest their potential into physical form in a world where our differences become our combined strength.

Chapter 42

PRINCIPLE 8: THE CONTRIBUTING

I choose to BE part of creating a world where every BE-ing can live out their Divine truth in, with and from freedom.

Expansion

This principle recognises every Truth-Walker's desire and Inspired action to create a world where every BE-ing feels safe and free to live in the Light of their deepest truth.

Meditation

Imagine standing with your bare feet on the ground in the middle of a forest. You can hear the soft bubbling of a stream in the distance and the call of birds. Life is pulsing all around you. In your hand is a length of string tied to a huge, red balloon filled with helium. You allow your body to feel light and, as the balloon floats in the wind, it tugs on your hand.

You feel your feet lifting off the ground and the balloon carries you higher – soon you are floating above the tall trees, blue sky surrounding you.

As you look down, you can see the stream winding its way through a path etched into the ground below. This stream becomes a bigger body of water as it meets other streams. Now it is a river meandering down the path with purpose. As you trace its route, you see it making its way to the ocean.

The ocean feels never-ending – would you know where one ocean ends and the next begins? Can you tell which water in the ocean is from which river? You feel the pitter-patter of raindrops on your skin. The droplets spill into the ocean, too. Is there any recognition of those droplets in the great ocean? Every droplet of water, whatever its origin, contributes and has a role to play – the ocean would not BE, without the contribution of the individual droplets of water.

As the rain comes down harder, you look upwards to your balloon. It is deflating gently, lowering you until your feet touch the ground again. As the rain nourishes the ground below your feet, feel your connection to Mother Earth, the water, and the sky above you. Feel the contribution of the water to your well-being, directly and indirectly. BE with this for a minute…

The essence

Just as each droplet of water contributes to the ocean, each of us contributes to our global collective consciousness. Our individuality allows each of us to contribute something unique. As Truth-Walkers, we are part of creating a world where every individual feels safe and free to contribute to our collective, and is appreciated for their contribution.

Inspired action

In the space you've created, be aware of your energy.

- What energy are you bringing to our world in this moment?
- What contribution are you making to our world through the reality you are creating in this moment?
- What do you want for our world?
- What do you feel called to contribute towards creating such a world?

Write down what comes to you in your journal. Know that as you raise your vibration, you are raising our world's vibration.

The meaning for your life

When you feel that your contribution is inconsequential in this big world, know that every drop of water gives the ocean meaning and contributes to its chemical properties and its movement. It is your vibration that creates a ripple effect and raises the collective vibration.

Just as one person's words can turn a crowd into a mob, your individual Light can have an impact on our world, and our collective Light can dissolve the darkness.

Part 6: GIVING

Chapter 43
DEAR TRUTH-WALKER

Dear Truth-Walker,

The truth is I didn't know how to end this book. Part 6 loomed over me, taunting me with excitement and truth. Why did I not simply write it? I came face-to-face with myself and realised I am teaching what I am still learning, what I believe all of us are still learning – to BE our truth at every level, in every space in our very full lives. Especially in the spaces between the full moments where we are completely vulnerable and empty – where the only feeling and sound present come from our own individual heartbeats.

I am creating these words right now and you are reading them and giving meaning to them. I have no preconceived ideas about where this path will take either of us, but I will open my Soul and trust that the words *will fall in the realm of my deepest intention. I will write my truth, no matter how vulnerable I feel. As I mentioned in Part 4: UN-Becoming, vulnerability is in the Rebirth Zone. It is a strength; the point where you are no longer in the space of insecurity about your truth.*

There will be no neatly formed feelings here. I am spilling out onto the page. Perhaps what I say will resonate with you or become the impetus for you taking a step forward on your journey. You and I have been connected in the pages of this book and I want that to continue – I want to speak to you directly here.

Have you ever been asked what the current version of you would say to your younger self when your younger self needed some love and direction? That question had me thinking about my eighteen or nineteen-year-old self. She felt tortured. She was the square peg being hammered into the round hole. Bits of her self-worth were chipped away with every blow. And she reached the point of despair – if she couldn't BE who she was inside, she didn't want to BE at all.

That young woman slept with a survival knife (a hunter's knife) under her bed where she could reach it so that, if she couldn't stand it anymore, she might have enough of what she called "courage" to end her pain. I am in gratitude that such a moment didn't come. I am proud of her for clinging to the original, fragile thread of who she was at her core and not giving in to existing as who she wasn't. I salute her for her warrior spirit and honour her journey. The beginning of that journey was her Point A. She has had many Point A's since then and reached many Point B's, each journey taking her to a place she needed to be. All the point A's and B's got her to her now.

Back to the question – what would I say to my nineteen-year-old self? I would tell her that the prison bars of circumstances and expectations that she saw around her were an illusion; that she was the one who had the power to wield the hammer, or to break it and BE the square peg.

I would tell her not to look for validation for who she was because there wasn't anyone who was in any way qualified to validate her truth. I'd let her know that her truth did not require approval and she should trust its message.

*I'd wish I could show her how okay she will be and how she will align with her deepest truth, know the power of her Inner Voice, find her tribe and even take up leadership in her tribe. I am not sure she'd believe me. That nineteen-year-old **me** didn't trust herself at all.*

Chapter 44
TRUST

It took me a long time to trust myself. After my lowest point, every choice was filled with fear that I would betray my trust; that I wouldn't value myself enough to keep any promise to myself – not even the promise to love and care for myself. But the trust comes when you give yourself permission to be YOU with no judgement from yourself.

Let's explore the trust issue. Do you trust yourself? If you are living in the Rebirth Zone at this moment, you are connected with your deepest truth and you feel a sense of trust in self. If you are not living in your deepest truth and you are in the Red Zone, you probably don't trust your opinions or your choices. It isn't your Point A that matters – you now know how to get to the Rebirth Zone if you're not there. The trust comes when you give yourself the space to connect with who you are. Trust in self comes first, then you feel the call to give who you are to the world.

Chapter 45
YOU AND THE COLLECTIVE

There are two principles that form the basis of contributing to your world:

- You are created in a world created by YOU.
- Wherever you go, there you are.

You are created in a world created by YOU

You create the world through your thoughts. Your thoughts give value to every life experience and every word and action that you know about in your world. Your perception is determined by that value. This world, created by you, is the world that continues to create and recreate every version of you throughout your evolution. Everything you have given importance to, becomes the world that continues to BE, in your experience of it. That is what you see and what your thoughts assign value to.

Wherever you go, there you are

As you learn to navigate this world, you are able to see yourself as participant and observer in your world. You realise that your life is not about the experiences but about what you take from these experiences; the significance you give to them. You get to decide who you will BE through each experience. As an observer, you realise that **wherever you go, there you are**. YOU are the common factor. You have the power to create your world, form your experiences, and, as observer, witness your creation. There are no prison bars holding you back except those that you accept into your experience.

The next step

So here we are: You are at the beginning. What is your next step? If you've undertaken the journey of a Truth-Walker, you know your truth. You have an awareness of your story. You've broken it down, you've taken the journey of seeking, you've UN-Become who you are not, and perhaps you're actively living by the Truth-Walker's Manifesto. Build from here. Build on the joy of BE-ing you. Do you feel you want to make a difference in your world?

The world can change on a dime – we see it changing before our eyes. Our collective priorities change; thoughts, words and actions collectively evolve. But the collective is made up of individuals. It is made up of you and I. If the collective can change so fast, it is a reflection of how fast we as individuals can shift our thoughts, words and actions; how quickly we can evolve and heal to our next level. We evolve fastest when there is an external reason – when we have to adapt to a new normal because we perceive that it is necessary for our survival.

What if we shift because we want to be connected to our deepest intentions? What if we shift to show up for ourselves first and, from that space, contribute to our collective shift? That would mean we no longer calibrate to the collective thinking as our default. We calibrate to our Source within (give it whatever name you want), and from that calibration we contribute the collective Light. We become the change we wish to see. We UN-Become who we are not as individuals and lead the UN-Becoming of our world so that every BE-ing feels safe and free to live out their Divine Truth.

Chapter 46
THE THOUGHT-SHIFT

Let's take this down a notch so it's not so pie-in-the-sky. What is this illusive shift and calibration, and how do we make it REAL?

We'll start with this question: What is your deepest intention? I'll define "intention" so that you have a guideline.

Intention – the thought-shift you wish to experience from any journey you are about to undertake.

Any activity you wish to use as a change-activator, can be classified as a journey. It could be watching a documentary, studying a personal growth book, keeping a gratitude journal, doing the exercises in *Part 2: Awareness* of this book, creating a default in thirty days (*Part 4: UN-Becoming*), or any other activity.

It is your deepest intention at your Point A that determines the direction of your Point B. If you have a deep desire to contribute to your world, start by showing up for YOU – find your deepest intention and choose your journey. It is this action that allows you to calibrate to Source within and BE the change you wish to see. It is from this energy space that you are contributing to the collective – your deepest truth forms part of the consciousness of our world. Know your deepest intention and align with your truth, and you will create your world as you wish to see it.

Chapter 47
THE LAST QUESTION

The only question left is: **what change do you wish to see in our world?**

Whatever that thought-shift is, BE it. Go on that journey of seeking. Create that default in thirty days. Do the energetic work, whatever it is. You matter. Your contribution to our collective makes a difference. You are the ripple effect in a world that is searching for your contribution. You are the thought-shift, the impetus, the activator, the catalyst.

Your capacity to receive this message and act on it is determined by whether you are living in the Rebirth Zone or not in this particular moment.

I hold the intention that you receive the message of how much your individual contribution to our world means, and that you act on it in whatever way you feel called. Take a breath with me in the space of this moment and join me in this intention...

May you create many moments of living in your deepest truth and your greatest sense of self-worth.

Namaste.

GIFT FOR YOU

Download your printable version of the Truth-Walker's Manifesto for you to align with your deepest intention daily and integrate the Manifesto into your way of BE-ing. It is lovingly designed by my sister. Download it here: truthwalkersjourney.com/manifesto

CONTINUE THE ADVENTURE – JOIN THE TRIBE

If you want a next step – a way of continuing the journey in the space of tribe – this may resonate.

Truth-Walker's Tribe is a space to:

- Heal to your next level in a global community.
- Connect and co-create in a space that is safe, rich with ideas, and infused with leading-edge growth.
- Participate in conscious conversations.
- Share ideas and exchange viewpoints.
- Enjoy meaningful messages from books and videos together.
- BE your aligned self in a space with other aligned BE-ings.

We welcome you to our community of pioneering-edge leaders, healers, deep listeners, and students of life who believe in personal sovereignty and living in joy – our *Truth-Walker's Tribe*. Wherever you are in the world, join our global community. I'm gifting you a 30-day free membership. Join here: truthwalkersjourney.com/gift

ACKNOWLEDGEMENTS

The journey of writing this book has been filled with emotion, Divine Inspiration, clarity, thought-shifts and experiences of pure Love. As Truth-Walker, I came face-to-face with my vulnerability, and watched the foundations of the beliefs that no longer served me, crumble. I felt called to stand in my Light and BE my truth. Between my Point A and B, I've been blessed by the presence of my tribe. I am in appreciation for their collective Light. To the people who helped and supported me as I breathed this book to life, I thank you:

My mom, Rashida Patel, comes first. She taught me to read when I was two years old and always supported my dream of being an author and poet (no one has nagged me more about getting this book out to the world than my mom!). My parents read to me and allowed me to explore new ideas and ways of BE-ing through the precious books they bought for me throughout my childhood. The love of words has stayed with me, and expressing my truth through writing has been my saving grace when I've felt disconnected from my Divinity. I am also in gratitude to my dad, Yacoob Patel, who is no longer on our Earthly plane. One of my fondest memories was when I was checking out a book from the library and the librarian commented that I wasn't allowed to take out an adult book with a "youth library card". My dad told her that I was allowed to read whatever I wanted to read, and the book came home with me!

Shameema Patel, my sister, believes in me much more than I believe in myself. She's brilliant and won't let me put out any writing to the world unless it's the best she believes I can offer – she has high standards. Her love and support makes me want to hug her constantly (except when we're having a disagreement). She's taught me what it means to create change in one's life and the world through a thought-shift – she's the epitome of a miracle, and one day I'll tell you why.

"I am more me because you are YOU" is the best way to describe how Tom Acklin's thought-provoking comments and questions have contributed to the evolution of both me and this book. He is my ever-present support in everything I do. He's read *The Truth-Walker's Journey* multiple times, has been through every exercise and has applied it practically.

Marty Humphreys, my "Other Mother" and writing coach has been with me as I progressed from writer to author. From our first hello, I knew she was going to be part of my life – it was one of those Divinely Inspired connections. I love her sense of humour and her art of saying it like it is, but with class and a good heart! I am honoured and grateful to have her edit this book. She was there for the Point A that became *The Truth-Walker's Journey*, and she's part of my Point B, which is so special.

Jennifer Skiff and I met in Perfect Divine Timing. I asked her to write a blurb for my book, and she called one Sunday morning because she believed so much in the message and potential of this book that she wanted to help me edit, despite her crazy schedule with her important global activism work for animal rights, and her many other projects. She's taught me how to be succinct and share what I mean in the most direct and receivable way possible.

My Deeptime family came into my life unexpectedly. In nine months, Jennifer Morgan's Deeptime Leadership program changed the trajectory of my life and my book! Stephan Martin, director of the Deeptime Leadership program contributed to this transformation. Sarbmeet Kanwal awakened my curiosity about cosmology in a way that related to individual human truth. Lisa Verni contributed her valuable insight as I brought this book to life. Lisa, Sarbmeet and I have had inspiring, eye-opening, conscious and uncomfortable conversations with love, differing viewpoints, respect and ease. That's how I feel the world should and can BE. Cami Flake gifted me by editing my photo for this book (Shameema took the picture with Cami's photography guidance). I have never been happier with a photo – it's my truth in a picture!

Working with Veronica Yager of YellowStudios to birth this book into the world has been a beautiful experience – the process flowed with ease and I am in gratitude.

To the rest of my tribe – you know who you are and how important you are to me. Thank you so much for so much. I appreciate the gift of having you in my life.

ABOUT THE AUTHOR

Haseena Patel is a healing breakthrough coach, author, international speaker, yoga instructor, Akashic Records reader, poet, certified Deeptime leader, and peace-builder from South Africa.

She works with clients globally to heal to their next evolutionary level through her Healing Breakthrough University.

She is also co-founder of Leave No Girl Behind International, a non-profit organisation that empowers girls worldwide through leadership programs.

Connect with Haseena through her websites:

https://truthwalkersjourney.com

https://haseenapatel.com

https://healingbreakthroughuniversity.com

https://leavenogirlbehind.org

And through social media:

https://www.facebook.com/haseena.patel.5

https://www.linkedin.com/in/haseenapateltruth-walker

https://www.instagram.com/hptruthwalker

Or email her directly at: hello@haseenapatel.com

www.ingramcontent.com/pod-product-compliance
Lightning Source LLC
Chambersburg PA
CBHW031244290426
44109CB00012B/430